THE GLORY OF THE LORD GOD ALMIGHTY

MARY L. HOCK

WESTBOW
PRESS®
A DIVISION OF THOMAS NELSON
& ZONDERVAN

WestBow Press books may be ordered through booksellers or by contacting:

WestBow Press
A Division of Thomas Nelson & Zondervan
1663 Liberty Drive
Bloomington, IN 47403
www.westbowpress.com
1 (866) 928-1240

Because of the dynamic nature of the Internet, any web addresses or links contained in this book may have changed since publication and may no longer be valid. The views expressed in this work are solely those of the author and do not necessarily reflect the views of the publisher, and the publisher hereby disclaims any responsibility for them.

Any people depicted in stock imagery provided by Thinkstock are models, and such images are being used for illustrative purposes only. Certain stock imagery © Thinkstock.

ISBN: 978-1-5127-3214-6 (sc)
ISBN: 978-1-5127-3213-9 (e)

Library of Congress Control Number: 2016903079

Print information available on the last page.

WestBow Press rev. date: 08/05/2016

CONTENTS

INTRODUCTION

I, Mary Lynelle Hock, do confess and acknowledge that Jesus Christ of Nazareth is my Savior and Lord for the past 50 plus years. I remember giving my heart to Jesus and making Him Lord of my life when I was just five years old in a little country church near my hometown of George, Iowa. I was blessed to grow up in a Christian home with family members and friends who were believers. He has been there for me for many years and He is my very best friend, Savior, deliverer, protector, provider, healer and much more! Thank you for dying on the cross for me, Lord! Thank you for all that Calvary means to me and the freedom I now have because of it. I am no longer a slave to sin, or held by any of Satan's strongholds and bondages, but I am a servant of Jesus Christ the Son of the God Almighty! He is master controller of my life and I desire to do His will. It is all about Him, not me. He must increase and I must decrease. I want to grow spiritually every day and see the glory of the Lord revealed to me on a regular basis. I love to be and abide in His presence.

Thank you Lord that I am free from all sin, condemnation, guilt, shame, unforgiveness, pain, sorrow, sickness, disease, infirmities, rejection, pride and jealousy and whatever else had me bound up! You, Lord, came to set the captives free from alcohol, drugs, nicotine, caffeine and any other thing that exalts itself above You, the Lord God Almighty. Blessed be the name of the Lord! Being in His presence helps me remain free from all these strongholds in my life!

Seth and I, along with Fred and Marcella Roark, were staying in Jerusalem for three months when God inspired me, by the power of the Holy Spirit who dwells in me, to start writing this book about the Presence of the Lord. He is the Creator of all things both great and small. I see God's glory everyday in His creation and creatures! Do you take the time to recognize and acknowledge God's glory through the people and things He has made?

In this book on the presence or glory of the Lord God Almighty, I will attempt with the help and anointing of the Holy Spirit to put into writing those things the Lord has deposited into my heart. I will discuss in the first chapter the meaning and purpose of His presence or glory. Then we will discover together how to enter into His presence and then how to stay or remain there according to the Bible. I will teach you how divine revelation comes to us when we are in the presence of the Lord. Then in chapter six we will learn how to stand in His presence. Then finally in the last chapter of this book on the presence or glory of the Lord God Almighty we will study, meditate, and acknowledge that Jesus is the King of glory. He is the glory!

Jesus of Nazareth walked in that glory realm while He was here on earth for three years during His public ministry and so can we. Jesus told us in John 14:12 KJV: "Verily, verily, I say unto you, He that believeth on me, the works that I do shall he do also; and greater works than these shall he do; because I go unto my Father." Jesus our Lord and Master went about all Israel and the surrounding area preaching, teaching and healing while in the presence of His Father in heaven and was anointed by the Holy Spirit to do so. Therefore, as His beloved children (sons and daughters) we have been chosen, anointed and equipped to follow in His footsteps and to say what He said and to do what He did and even greater things. For what purpose did God Almighty create us? To bring glory and honor to our heavenly Father and to His Son and to be blessed by the Lord and be a blessing to others while here on this planet. Also, it is our job to help as many people as we possibly can along the adventure or journey until we obtain our ultimate goal which is to make heaven our home some day. We could go by the grave or we could go in the Rapture, only God Almighty knows this about us.

When God created man and woman (mankind) His primary purpose was to have fellowship with him or her. He desired that the lives of men and women would bring glory and honor unto Him, their maker. My daily prayer is that everything I say and do these days would bring glory and honor unto Him. Do I accomplish this every day? I do not, but some days are better than others, and for that I am grateful and thankful. I also recognize that I need the Lord's help each and every day to walk in the spirit and not fulfill the desires of my flesh. The desire of my heart is to walk in the anointing He has placed upon me, to do His will, to remain meek and humble, to enjoy one day at a time, not to be concerned or worry about all my tomorrows, and to get and remain in the glory realm as much and as often as He allows. Thank you Lord for all that you have done for me and through me and thank you in advance for all that you are going to continue to do and even more. Thank you for the cross, thank you for Your blood, thank you for Your love, and thank you for Calvary for all you did and all that was accomplished there for me and for all who read this book now and forever. Amen!

CHAPTER ONE

The Presence and Glory of the Lord

The Meaning of His Presence and Glory

When the Bible talks about the presence and glory of the Lord, it is referring to seeing the splendor and glory of our Lord in a visible sense.

Webster's New World Dictionary, College Edition defines *presence* as:
1. Immediate surroundings; vicinity within close view; as in, "I was admitted into his presence";
2. Attendance, company;
3. An influence or supernatural spirit felt to be present such as the presence of the Lord through the Holy Spirit.

Webster defines *glory* as:
1. Great honor and admiration won by doing something important or valuable; fame; renowned;
2. Worship; adoration; praise;
3. Splendor, magnificence; radiance;
4. Heaven or the bliss of heaven;
5. Glorified to be very proud; rejoice, exult.

We are to glorify or worship the Lord and Him alone. Men or women are not to be glorified—only God, Jesus, and the Holy Spirit are to be glorified. Almighty God, the Trinity, deserves all of our praise, honor, and He alone is to be glorified, no one else!

The Manifestation of His Glory

Concerning God, glory is the display of His divine attributes and perfection. Concerning man, glory is the manifestation of His commendable qualities such as wisdom, righteousness, self-control, ability, etc. *Splendid*, *marvelous*, *outstanding*, *excellent*, and *supernatural* are terms that pertain to things that God Almighty created: "The sun has one kind of splendor, the moon another and the stars another; and star differs from star in splendor" (1 Corinthians 15:41 NIV). The NLT says, "The sun has one kind of glory, while the moon and stars each have another kind."

God displays His glory through what he created! Even the stars differ from each other in their beauty and brightness. Isn't it truly amazing that all the stars and also the snowflakes each have their own unique qualities? Not one of them is exactly the same. Likewise, we as God's children differ one from another, each having been given by God Almighty unique or special skills, talents, or gifts. The glory of the Lord God Almighty can be seen in His creation—both in earthly things and in mankind! Are you taking the time to see the glory of the Lord God Almighty?

The Shekinah Glory of God Almighty

In both the Old and the New Testaments, there are references to the Shekinah glory of God (although not by name, for the word occurs in the Targums, not in the Bible). The Targums are any of several translations or paraphrases or parts of the Old Testament, written in the vernacular (Aramaic) of Judea. Targum writers spoke of the glory of the Shekinah.

Shekinah was actually the physical manifestation of the presence of God as seen in the Old Testament as pillars of cloud by day and pillars of fire by night. New Testament references to the *Shekinah* glory are seen in John 1:4 and Romans 9:4.

Glory is both physical and spiritual, as is seen in Luke 2:9 and John 17:22, where it refers to the glory of the Father, which Jesus gave to His disciples before he left the earth to be with His heavenly Father forever.

As for the saints of God, life culminates in the changing of their bodies to the likeness of their glorified Lord. "But we are citizens of heaven, where the Lord Jesus Christ lives. And we are eagerly waiting for Him to return as our Savior. He will take these weak mortal bodies of ours and change them into glorious bodies like His own, using the same mighty power that he will use to conquer everything, everywhere" (Philippians 3:20–21 NLT). Moses and Aaron told the Israelites that they would see the presence of the Lord in Exodus 16:7: "In the morning you will see the glorious **presence of the LORD**" (NLT, *emphasis added*). The NKJV says "the glory of the Lord." In the Old Testament when the Israelites were led out of Egypt by Moses there were times when they saw the glory of the Lord as shown in these Scripture references:

- Exodus 16:10: "Now it came to pass, as Aaron spoke to the whole congregation of the children of Israel, that they looked toward the wilderness, and behold, the glory of the LORD appeared in the cloud."
- Exodus 24:17: "The sight of the glory of the LORD was like a consuming fire on the top of the mountain in the eyes of the children of Israel."
- Exodus 40:34–35: "Then the cloud covered the Tabernacle, and the glorious presence of the LORD filled it" (NLT). The KJV says, "The glory of the LORD filled the tabernacle." Moses was no longer able to enter the Tabernacle because the cloud had settled down over it, and the Tabernacle was filled with the awesome glory of the LORD.
- Leviticus, 9:23: "Next Moses and Aaron went into the Tabernacle, and when they came back out, they blessed the people again, and the glorious presence of the LORD appeared to the whole community" (NLT). The NKJV says, "Then the glory of the LORD appeared to all the people."
- Numbers 16:32: "As the people gathered to protest to Moses and Aaron, they turned toward the Tabernacle and saw that the cloud had covered it, and the glorious presence of the LORD appeared" (NLT). The NKJV says, "the glory of the LORD appeared."
- 1 Kings 8:11: "The priests could not continue their work because the glorious presence of the LORD filled the Temple" (NLT).

But the Israelites were not the only ones who saw the glory or presence of the Lord. Solomon, the priests and all the people of Israel also experienced and saw the same awesome presence of God in 2 Chronicles 7:1–3: "When Solomon finished praying, fire flashed down from heaven and burned up the burnt offerings and sacrifices, and the glorious **presence of the LORD** filled the Temple. The priests could not even enter the Temple of the LORD because the glorious **presence of**

the LORD filled it. When all the people of Israel saw the fire coming down and the glorious **presence of the LORD** filling the Temple, they fell face down on the ground and worshiped and praised the LORD, saying, "He is so good! His faithful love endures forever" (NLT)! "When all the children of Israel saw how the fire came down, and the **glory of the LORD** filled the temple, they all fell down on their faces to praise and worship their Lord" (verse 3 NKJV, emphasis added).

We see from these scriptures that the children of Israel saw the presence or glory of God many times. They experienced and saw with their own eyes the glory of God. We need to see the glory of the Lord. But do we desire and pursue this? In these last days God will reveal Himself by His glory. The glory of the Lord will be shown to us in supernatural ways. Even nature does and will proclaim His glory. God has revealed Himself in the past through many natural occurrences such as earthquakes, hurricanes, floods, famines, tornadoes, etc. The nation of Israel has seen God's hand of protection upon them through supernatural acts of nature many times throughout the history of this great nation. Explain to me how a little country the size of one of USA's smallest states could survive all the wars and struggles they have gone through if God's hand of protection were not upon them. God is watching over and taking care of His people and His nation Israel. Woe be unto those nations who rise up against them because God said in Genesis 12:3: "I will bless those who bless you and curse those who curse you. All the families of the earth will be blessed through you" (NLT). Throughout the history of God's people, the Israelites, God has totally annihilated nations who have risen up against them. He is well able to do the same today. God will defend, protect and preserve His nation—the land He gave to Abraham, Isaac, and Jacob forever. Man is not capable of bringing peace to Israel. Sign all the peace treaties you want to, but peace will be accomplished there only when its people's eyes are unveiled and they receive Jesus as the Prince of Peace.

What does King David tells us to do in Psalm 37:7–9? "Be still in the presence of the LORD, and wait patiently for Him to act. Don't worry about evil people who prosper or fret about their wicked schemes. Stop your anger! Turn from your rage! Do not envy others it only leads to harm. For the wicked will be destroyed, but those who trust in the LORD will possess the land" (NLT). David is telling us to rest in the presence of the Lord and wait patiently for Him to do what needs to be done in your life or your country. He tells us not to worry or fret about evil people and their plans! We are told by King David to let God take care of our enemies. He will destroy those who rise up against us. We don't have to retaliate or get even. He concludes by telling us that those who wait or trust in the Lord will possess or inherit the earth. God will destroy the wicked or those who do evil to us. We don't have to do anything except trust God and wait on the Lord to give us our inheritance. Too many times we try to fix things ourselves which is not what the Word of God tells us to do.

God will also return to His children, the children of Israel, their land—their inheritance that rightfully belongs to them. God gave it to them and no man can take it from them. All the land God gave them when they came to the Middle East will be returned to them including the areas which the tribes of Reuben, Gad, and the half tribe of Manasseh possessed, which are now in Jordan. God has made an everlasting covenant with the children of Israel that this land is their inheritance. Just take a look at Genesis 13:14–15: "And the LORD said unto Abram, after that Lot was separated from him, Lift up now thine eyes, and look from the place where thou art northward, and southward, and eastward, and westward: For all the land which thou seest, to thee will I give it, and to thy seed **forever**" (emphasis added). In this passage, the Lord told Father Abraham that this land belonged to him and his children forever. God hasn't changed His mind. It is still their land and it will always be their land.

The Ark of the Covenant

The Ark of God contained three things:
- The original ten commandment tablets that God gave Moses on Mt. Sinai,
- Aaron's rod which had budded and
- Manna.

The Word of God has a lot to say about the Ark of the Covenant of God. Refer to 1 Samuel 4:1–11 to read about how the Philistines captured the Ark of God and took it from Shiloh to Ashdod. Also the account in 1 Samuel 5:1–5 tells what happened to the Philistine god Dagon when they put the Ark of God next to him, which is quite interesting and even amusing. The NLT says in verses 6–8:

> Then the LORD began to afflict the people of Ashdod and the nearby villages with a plague of tumors. When the people realized what was

happening, they cried out, "We can't keep the Ark of the God of Israel here any longer! He is against us! We will all be destroyed along with our god Dagon." So they called together the rulers of the five Philistine cities and asked, "What should we do with the Ark of the God of Israel?" The rulers discussed it and replied, "Move it to the city of Gath." So they moved the Ark of the God of Israel to Gath.

Again the Ark of God was moved from Gath to Ekron. They did not want the ark either, because those who did not die were afflicted with tumors also. The Ark of God remained in Philistine territory seven months. Then the Philistines decided to send the Ark back to Israel. (Read about this account in 1 Samuel 6:2–19.) The ark was sent to Beth-shemesh, where seventy men were killed because they looked into the Ark of the Lord (verse 19). The Philistines were the ones who came up with the idea to put the ark on a new cart and have it carried by cows. This is not how God had told the Israelites to transport the Ark of God. So the people of Beth-shemesh did not want the ark either.

> "Who is able to stand in the presence of the LORD, this holy God?" they cried out. "Where can we send the Ark from here?" So they sent messengers to the people at Kiriath-jearim and told them, "The Philistines have returned the Ark of the LORD. Please come here and get it!" So the men of Kiriath-jearim came to get the Ark of the LORD. They took it to the hillside home of Abinadab and ordained Eleazar, his son, to be in charge of it. The Ark remained in Kiriath-jearim for a long time—twenty years in all. During that time, all Israel mourned because it seemed that the LORD had abandoned them (1 Samuel 6:20–7:2 NLT).

So during the time that the ark was not possessed by the Israelites, they felt as if the presence of the Lord had left them. The Ark of the Covenant of God was the tangible presence of the Lord to His people, the Israelites. King David brought the Ark of God back to Shiloh but an incident happened in which Uzzah reached out to catch the ark when the cart became unstable and the ark was going to fall to the ground; and Uzzah died. (Refer to 2 Samuel 6:2–10 for this account.) In 2 Samuel 6:10–12, NLT we find out what David decided to do with the Ark of God:

So David decided not to move the Ark of the LORD into the City of David. Instead, he took it to the house of Obed-edom of Gath. The Ark of the LORD remained there in Obed-edom's house for three months, and the LORD blessed Obed-edom and his entire household. Then King David was told, "The LORD has blessed Obed-edom's household and everything he has because of the Ark of God." So David went there and brought the Ark of God from the house of Obed-edom to the City of David with a great celebration.

This time they transported the Ark of God the way it was supposed to be carried—by the priests. King David embarrassed his wife Michal by dancing before the Lord with all his might in just a linen ephod (priestly tunic). (2 Samuel 6:14). "The Ark of the LORD was placed inside a special tent that David had prepared for it. And David sacrificed burnt offerings and peace offerings to the LORD" (2 Samuel 16:17). "When the king was settled in his palace and the LORD had brought peace to the land, David summoned Nathan the prophet. 'Look!' David said. 'Here I am living in this beautiful cedar palace, but the Ark of God is out in a tent!'"(2 Samuel 7:1–2 NLT). So because King David was getting old, the Lord told him that his son Solomon would build a temple to house the Ark of the Covenant of God and that is where the Ark of God remained for many years!

This Biblical account about the Ark of God is very interesting to me because it shows how very important the Ark of the Covenant was to God's people and how it represented the tangible presence of the Lord wherever it was! The Israelites believed that wherever the Ark of God was that His presence dwelt there also. When the temple which Solomon built was destroyed, the Ark of God was lost or hidden. I believe someday when the time is right the Ark of the Covenant of God will be rediscovered in its original condition.

Are You Being Refreshed by the Presence of God or Are You Hiding from His Presence?

Paul tells us in Acts 3:19 that we are refreshed by being in the presence of the Lord. "Repent therefore and be converted, that your sins may be blotted out, so that times of refreshing may come from the presence of the Lord." The NLT says "wonderful times of refreshment will come from the **presence of the Lord**" (emphasis added).

We all need those times of refreshing. Thank God for them. While we were in the Middle East for three months in the year 2000, we were refreshed as we experienced and entered into the presence of the Lord. It had been prophesied to us that we would bring the glory of the Lord back with us to Columbus, Ohio. I believe that we did! Immediately upon arriving in Israel, we could sense the presence of the Lord upon that country!

In Genesis 3:8, we see Adam and his wife Eve hid themselves from the presence of the Lord God: "And they heard the sound of the LORD God walking in the garden in the cool of the day, and Adam and his wife hid themselves from the presence of the LORD God among the trees of the garden." Why did they hide from the presence of the Lord? They had disobeyed God by eating of the tree of life and after this fall into sin their communion with God was affected. Before they fell into sin and disobeyed God, they walked and talked with God and were in His presence on a daily basis. Adam walked and talked with God in the cool of the day. He was in the presence of the Lord all the time. If the presence of the Lord left them because of disobedience then, how do you think we can get back into the presence of the Lord?

Do you hide from the presence of the Lord or are you refreshed by it? Because Adam and Eve were disobedient to God Almighty, they were put out of the garden and then banned from the presence of the Lord. So if disobedience separates us from His presence, then perhaps by being obedient to the Word of God and being sensitive to the leading of the Holy Spirit we can regain the honor of entering into His presence. We will discuss how we enter into His presence in chapter three.

Characteristics of the Glory of the Lord and His Presence

The Glory of the Lord Lasts Forever

David tells us in Psalm 104:31, "May the glory of the LORD last forever! The LORD rejoices in all he has made" (NLT)! The glory of the Lord can last forever and the Bible tells us that the Lord rejoices in everything He has made. We can see the glory of the Lord in His creation—God created many marvelous and wonderful things and places. We are also fearfully and wonderfully made. I will explore this further in the next chapter.

There is Fullness of Joy in the Presence of the Lord

In Psalm 16:11, David talks about how we can have fullness of joy in His presence. "You will show me the path of life; In Your **presence** is fullness of joy; At Your right hand are pleasures forevermore" (emphasis added). When we get into the presence of the Lord we will be full of the joy of the Lord, which will give us strength (Nehemiah 8:10). Believers should be the most blessed, happy people on the face of this earth. Our countenance should radiate the joy of the Lord—so does it? Unbelievers should admire and want what we have! The fruit of the spirit as we walk in the spirit and not the flesh should be manifested in our lives—is it? Again King David says in Psalm 68: 3–4, to rejoice in His presence. "But let the godly rejoice. Let them be glad in God's presence. Let them be filled with joy. Sing praises to God and to his name! Sing loud praises to him who rides the clouds. His name is the LORD—**rejoice in his presence!**" (NLT, emphasis added).

The Glory of the Lord is Great

David also speaks of how great the glory of the Lord is. In Psalm 138:5 he says, "For I know that the LORD is great, and our Lord is above all gods." The Lord is very great and His glory is great also. If you have ever experienced being in His presence when the glory falls, you would agree with me that nothing on earth compares with being in that glory realm. We need to seek after that glory. We need to experience the glory of the Lord for ourselves. Great and mighty things happen in the glory realm.

While in Jerusalem, Nancy Bergen taught us that there are three realms here on earth: the carnal realm, the faith realm, and the glory realm. Most of us live in the carnal realm too much of the time because we don't spend enough time with the Lord, fellowshipping with Him. We spend most of our time doing carnal activities. Thus, we remain in the carnal realm most of the time. Then we think we have arrived when we get into the faith realm, but we need to press on until we advance spiritually into the glory realm, which is like being in heaven. The glory realm is a little bit of heaven on earth. Perhaps, like me, you have been privileged to be in this glory realm from time to time. Nothing here on earth comes close to or can be compared to the awesome ***presence and glory of the Lord God Almighty.***

The Glory of the Lord Will be Revealed

The prophet Isaiah prophesied to us that the glory of the Lord would be revealed to us in Isaiah 40:4–5: "Fill the valleys and level the hills. Straighten out the curves and smooth off the rough spots. Then the **glory of the LORD** will be revealed, and all people will see it together. The LORD has spoken!" (NLT, emphasis added). If we do our part by straightening out the curves and smoothing off the rough spots in our lives—live a holy life and walk in holiness—then the glory of the Lord will be revealed to us. We will all see it together as we assemble to praise and worship the Lord. In these last days the glory of the Lord is being revealed to the body of Christ individually and corporately.

The Glory of the Lord is Our Rear Guard

Isaiah prophesied to us in Isaiah 58:8 that the glory of the Lord would be our rear guard. Isaiah also prophesied over Israel in Isaiah 60:1–5, saying, "Arise, Jerusalem! Let your light shine for all the nations to see! For the **glory of the LORD** is shining upon you. Darkness as black as night will cover all the nations of the earth, but the **glory of the LORD** will shine over you. All nations will come to your light. Mighty kings will come to see your radiance. Look and see, for everyone is coming home! Your sons are coming from distant lands; your little daughters will be carried home. Your eyes will shine, and your hearts will thrill with joy, for merchants from around the world will come to you. They will bring you the wealth of many lands" (NLT, emphasis added). The glory of the Lord is shining upon Israel. He is revealing Himself to the Jewish people there and they are seeing Jesus walking the streets of Jerusalem. They are His people, and His glory is shining all over that land. While we were in Israel and the surrounding area for three months in the year 2000, we saw many wonderful and spectacular places where God revealed His glory to us. There is an awesome presence of the Lord in that land that you can feel the minute you get there.

The Glory of the Lord is Revealed through His Creations

We learned much about the land of Israel and the people by being there for three months. Seth and I had been to Israel as tourists once before for ten days in 1993, but when we spent three months there it was a whole new and deeper experience. God allowed us to visit not only Jerusalem and the surrounding areas of Israel, but we went to Greece, Egypt, and Jordan also. While in Jordan we stayed with Doctor Batarseh and His wife Nina. He took us to see many wonderful places in Jordan. Petra and Mount Nebo were two of my favorite places. There is nowhere in the whole world that compares to them; not only because of their beauty but also because of their spectacular demonstration of God's presence. I felt like Mount Nebo was the most holy place we visited while in the Middle East. While we were there the Lord opened up my eyes to see many wonderful things through His acts of nature and in His Word that I didn't see before. The Word of God became alive and I got to see many of the places and things mentioned in the Bible. Take time to see God not only in His Word but through things and places He has created. God has a way of revealing His glory through what He created. We serve a great and mighty God and His greatness and glory are revealed by the places and things He has made. In Psalm 19:1–6, David talks about how the heavens declare the glory of God: "The heavens tell of the glory of God. The skies display His marvelous craftsmanship. Day after day they continue to speak; night after night they make him known. They speak without a sound or a word; their voice is silent in the skies; yet their message has gone out to all the earth, and their words to the entire world. The sun lives in the heavens where God placed it. It bursts forth like a radiant bridegroom after His wedding. It rejoices like a great athlete eager to run the race. The sun rises at one end of the heavens and follows its course to the other end. Nothing can hide from its heat" (NLT). I see the glory or splendor of God in a sunrise or a sunset. Do you take the time to see and acknowledge God's glory when the sun rises or when it sets?

The Future Glory of the Lord

Ezekiel described the glory of the Lord in Ezekiel 1:1–28. Verse 27 of the NLT says, "From his waist up, he looked like gleaming amber, flickering like a fire. And from his waist down, he looked like a burning flame, shining with splendor. All around him was a glowing halo, like a rainbow shining through the clouds. This was the way **the glory of the LORD** appeared to me. When I saw it, I fell face down in the dust" (emphasis added). Through this vision God showed Ezekiel His glory.

Another way He reveals Himself is through visions and dreams. This was prophesied by Joel, in Joel 2:28: "And it shall come to pass afterward That I will pour out My Spirit on all flesh; Your sons and your daughters shall prophesy, Your old men shall dream dreams, Your young men shall see visions." This prophesy is being fulfilled through the Holy Spirit in this generation!

11

The prophet Habakkuk tells us in Habakkuk 2:14: *"For the time will come when all the earth will be filled, as the waters fill the sea, with an awareness of the **glory of the LORD"*** (NLT, emphasis added). I believe that this prophecy is being fulfilled in this generation also. More and more people are becoming aware and seeing the glory of the Lord. In the last few months I have become more aware of the glory of the Lord all around me and I am expecting God to reveal more and more of His glory to me. My desire is to see the glory of the Lord with my visible eyes. I believe God will do that for me through visions, dreams, or being present when His glory falls on the body of Christ. In 2 Corinthians 3:17–18, the NLT tells us, "Now, the Lord is the Spirit, and wherever the Spirit of the Lord is, he gives freedom. And all of us have had that veil removed so that we can be mirrors that brightly reflect the **glory of the Lord"** (emphasis added). As the Spirit of the Lord works within us, we become more and more like Him and reflect His glory even more. Others will see the glory of the Lord in our countenance and our appearance.

His glory will be revealed to others through us. Ruth Ward Heflin speaks of the glory of the Lord as appearing as gold dust in her meetings in her *Glory* books. It is my desire to be present someday when this glory dust falls. I want to experience the glory of God in this way. What about you? Do you want to experience God's glory too? Do you want to see the glory of the Lord with your own eyes? We can and we will. The Bible tells us that when Moses came down from Mount Moriah with the two stone tablets in his hands, the Israelites visibly saw the glory of the Lord on Moses' face (Exodus 24, 33:13–23; 34:28–30). Will we ever see this kind of glory again? I pray that we do! I want to see that kind of glory on people's faces, don't you? I believe it can and will happen in the last days as we desire and seek His Shekinah!

Conclusion

In this chapter, we discovered the meaning of the presence and glory of the Lord. We learned about the Shekinah glory of God and where it is found. We saw how the Israelites visibly and spiritually experienced the glory of God and how David also talked about this same glory in the Psalms. The prophets of the Old Testament spoke of this glory and we can experience this same glory in our lives today!

Chapter One

Review Questions

1. Give me Webster's definition of the word *presence*:

2. Give me Webster's definition of the word *glory*:

3. Where is the word *Shekinah* found and what does it mean?

4. Give three Old Testament references that show that the Israelites saw or experienced the glory of God.
    1.)
    2.)
    3.)

5. Does God reveal His glory or presence through nature—what he has created? If so give at least three examples to support your answer.
    1.)
    2.)
    3.)

6. What does King David tell us to do in Psalm 37:7–9 (NLT)?

7. Has God made an everlasting covenant with the children of Israel that has made the Land of Israel their inheritance? If so, give the Scripture reference to support your answer.

8. Paul tells us in _____ that we are refreshed by being in the presence of the Lord. How does the presence of God refresh you?

9. David tells us in Psalm 104:31 (NLT) "may the glory of the Lord last _____. Does it last that long? If not, why not?

10. In Psalm 16:11 David talks about how we can have _____ of joy in His presence. Have you ever experienced this? When and how?

11. Again David says in Psalm 68:3–4 to _____ in His presence. It would be good for us to memorize these verses of Scripture! Put them on a note card and keep these words somewhere in front of you.

12. Have you ever experienced being in the glory realm? If so, what happens or takes place in the glory realm?

13. The prophet Isaiah prophesied to us that the glory of the Lord would be revealed to us in _____. Write out this Scripture and meditate on it for a few minutes.

14. Isaiah also prophesied in Isaiah 58:8 that the glory of the Lord would be our _____.

15. In what ways do the heavens declare the glory of God according to King David in Psalm 19:1–6?

16. In what ways did Ezekiel describe the glory of our Lord in Ezekiel 1:1–28, especially verse 27?

17. Who told us in the Old Testament that God would reveal Himself through visions and dreams? Write out this Scripture and memorize it.

18. The prophet Habakkuk tells us in verse 2:14 that "the time will come when all the earth will be filled, as the waters fill the sea, with an awareness of the glory of the Lord." Do you believe that this prophecy is being fulfilled in our generation? If so, why?

CHAPTER TWO

God Demonstrates His Glory and Presence in Many Wonderful Ways

Review of Chapter One

In chapter one, we discussed the meaning of His presence and glory. I shared with you the information I have concerning the Shekinah glory of God Almighty. We saw in the Old Testament Scriptures how God revealed His glory to the Israelites almost every day as they journeyed towards the Promised Land and wandered in the wilderness. The Ark of the Covenant of God represented the tangible presence of the Lord. I talked to you about how we can be refreshed by or hide from the presence of the Lord. We can have fullness of joy in His presence and His glory can last forever! We closed chapter one by discussing how the Lord will reveal His glory in the future.

God Displays His Glory in Many Ways

The glory of the Lord appears to us in many spectacular ways through God's own creation. Some common ways in which God Almighty displays His glory are:

1. A sunrise or sunset
2. A rainbow-half ones, whole ones, double ones
3. A storm of any kind such as a tornado, a hurricane, a thunderstorm, an earthquake, a sand storm, a snow storm-blizzard, a tsunami, these storms demonstrate the fierceness and power of our Lord.
4. The stars, moon, sun, and planets in the heaven that we can see with our naked eye.

- Psalm 50:6: "And the heavens proclaim his righteousness, for God himself is judge. Selah" (NIV).
- Romans 1:18–25: "But God shows his anger from heaven against all sinful, wicked people who push the truth away from themselves. For the truth about God is known to them instinctively. God has put this knowledge in their hearts. From the time the world was created, people have seen the earth and sky and all that God made. They can clearly see his invisible qualities--his eternal power and divine nature. So they have no excuse whatsoever for not knowing God. Yes, they knew God, but they wouldn't worship him as God or even give him thanks. And they began to think up foolish ideas of what God was like. The result was that their minds became dark and confused. Claiming to be wise, they became utter fools instead. And instead of worshiping the glorious, ever-living God, they worshiped idols made to look like mere people, or birds and animals and snakes. So God let them go ahead and do whatever shameful things their hearts desired. As a result, they did vile and degrading things with each other's bodies. Instead of believing what they knew was the truth about God; they deliberately chose to believe lies. So they worshiped the things God made but not the Creator himself, who is to be praised forever" (NLT). Amen. God Almighty desires that we worship Him, not those things He created for us to enjoy.

Nature Displays the Awesome Handiwork of our Lord

Psalm 19:1: "The heavens declare the glory of God; and the firmament shows His handiwork." The NLT says, "The heavens tell of the glory of God. The skies display his marvelous craftsmanship."

In the Dew, the Fog, and Icicles

- Psalms 147:16–18: "He sends the snow like white wool; he scatters frost upon the ground like ashes. He hurls the hail like stones. Who can stand against his freezing cold? Then, at his command, it all melts. He sends his winds, and the ice thaws" (NLT).
- Psalms 148:7–13.: "Praise the LORD from the earth, you creatures of the ocean depths, fire and hail, snow and storm, wind and weather that obey him, mountains and all hills, fruit trees and all cedars, wild animals and

all livestock, reptiles and birds, kings of the earth and all people, rulers and judges of the earth, young men and maidens, old men and children. Let them all praise the name of the LORD. For his name is very great; his glory towers over the earth and heaven" (NLT)!

The Bible speaks of our sins being washed away and our hearts becoming as white and pure as new fallen snow. Isaiah 1:18 says, "Come now; let us argue this out," says the LORD. "No matter how deep the stain of your sins, I can remove it. I can make you as clean as freshly fallen snow. Even if you are stained as red as crimson, I can make you as white as wool" (NLT).

In the Animals, Plants and Trees

We can see the glory and splendor or our Maker in the many different species of birds, fish, insects, and mammals that God has created for our pleasure and use. How intricately and precisely they function as each one has its own purpose.

All the many different natural or wild plants, trees, and flowers that grow on this earth in various parts of the world reveal to us how glorious is our Lord! All are unique and specific for the area or place where they grow. Each displays their grandeur and splendor—a reflection of God's creativeness and glory!

In the Seasons of the Year, and the Sunrise and Sunset

Here in Ohio we have four seasons: spring, summer, fall, and winter. Each season displays its own beauty and has a specific purpose, but for me fall is when the Lord shows us how great and awesome He really is: when the leaves change colors in brilliant varieties of red, gold, and orange. That is my favorite time of the year! I see and realize how creative and magnificent our God is by the different seasons He has blessed us with.

Nature in general reveals the glory of our Lord-He paints a picture of His greatness and magnificence every day by revealing Himself through nature, a sunrise or a sunset. So take the time to enjoy, appreciate and be thankful for what God has created and see and acknowledge His presence and creative ability through what His hands have made.

- Colossians 1:16–17: "Christ is the one through whom God created everything in heaven and earth. He made the things we can see and the things we can't see, kings, kingdoms, rulers, and authorities. Everything has been created through him and for him. He existed before everything else began, and he holds all creation together" (NLT).
- 1 Timothy 1:4: "Since everything God created is good," Our God is a good God and everything He created is good. His creation is a display of His beauty and glory" (NLT)!
- Isaiah 45:5–8: "I am the LORD, and there is no other; Besides Me there is no God. I will gird you, though you have not known me; that men may know from the rising to the setting of the sun that there is no one besides me. I am the LORD, and there is no other, The One forming light and creating darkness, causing well-being and creating calamity; I am the LORD who does all these. "Drip down, O heavens, from above, And let the clouds pour down righteousness; Let the earth open up and salvation bear fruit, And righteousness spring up with it. I, the LORD, have created it" (NASB).

Our Human Bodies Display the Glory of the Lord

I believe we can even see the glory and wonder of our Lord in our own earthly vessels or bodies. Our physical bodies are so intricately designed and consist of so many delicate and functional parts each with its own purpose to make the whole body to function and perform just the way it was intended to perform or function. Each tiny little cell, organ, tissue, bone, or muscle functioning just the way God made it to perform. Our brains are a very complex computer formed by the hands of an Almighty Father! Each and every organ is very intricate and man is not able to duplicate what our Maker created.

- Psalm 139:14 tells us that we are fearfully and wonderfully made, or one translation says wonderfully complex.
- Isaiah 45:9–12: "Woe to the one who quarrels with his Maker—An earthenware vessel among the vessels of earth! Will the clay say to the potter, 'What are you doing?' Or the things you are making say, 'He has no hands?' Woe to him who says to a father, 'What are you begetting?' Or to a woman, 'To what are you giving birth?' Thus says the LORD, the Holy One of Israel, and his Maker: 'Ask Me about the things to come concerning my sons, and

you shall commit to me the work of my hands. It is I who made the earth, and created man upon it. I stretched out the heavens with my hands, and I ordained their entire host'" (NASB).

- Isaiah 45:9–12: "Destruction is certain for those who argue with their Creator. Does a clay pot ever argue with its maker? Does the clay dispute with the one who shapes it, saying, 'Stop, you are doing it wrong?' Does the pot exclaim, 'How clumsy can you be?' How terrible it would be if a newborn baby said to its father and mother, 'Why was I born? Why did you make me this way? This is what the LORD, the Creator and Holy One of Israel, says: "Do you question what I do? Do you give me orders about the work of my hands? I am the one who made the earth and created people to live on it. With my hands I stretched out the heavens. All the millions of stars are at my command" (NLT).

Each one of us has unique body features and our bodies are so complex and each part of our bodies has specific functions so that the whole body can perform like it should. We are fearfully and wonderfully made by a Creator who loves us and made each one of us to be unique and special in His eyes.

Therefore, because our bodies are the temple of the Holy Spirit and the Spirit of God resides inside of our bodies, we should take care of this temple and respect it. Ezekiel 37:1–10 tells us that before God breathed life into us we were just a bunch of dead bones.

- 1 Corinthians 6:19–20: "Do you not know that your body is a temple of the Holy Spirit, who is in you, whom you have received from God? You are not your own; you were bought at a price. Therefore honor God with your body" (NIV).
- 1 Corinthians 2:16–17: "Do you not know that you are a temple of God, and that the Spirit of God dwells in you? If any man destroys the temple of God, God will destroy him, for the temple of God is holy, and that is what you are" (NASB).

Since our bodies are the temple or tabernacle of the Holy Spirit, we should treat them with great respect and honor, and not misuse or abuse our bodies in any way. If you are a person who does not love your own body, the way God created you, then, I believe that you are saying to the Father that you do not approve of or like what He created. I remember a time in my own life when I did not love myself, I did not like my nose, my hair, my physic, and one day I was complaining to God about it. He said to me in a still small voice that He made my nose, the color of my hair, my body parts and that my body was fearfully and wonderfully made, designed by Him—one of a kind. He was telling me that if I didn't love myself and appreciate how He made me then I was insulting Him and, more or less, telling Him that I did not like what He created. Since that time I have come to accept, and love myself just the way I am—what you see is what you get! God doesn't make any junk. We are all His children and we are all fearfully and wonderfully made. We get so hung up on our appearance—how we look, the color of our hair, the length of our hair, the shape of our body, our physical features. Yes, these things should be important to us, because they are important to God our Maker or Creator, but we should not be consumed or overly concerned about them to the point where we spend more time on improving these things about ourselves and we fail to concentrate on what really is important to us, like the condition of our hearts and our relationship with our Lord and with others.

The Condition and Attitudes of Our Heart

Do you spend more time in front of the mirror making your body more beautiful or in my case presentable than you do reading your Word, praying, spending time with God that day? Are you more concerned about your outward beauty than you are your inner beauty-the condition of your heart (the attitudes of your heart)? What does the Word of God have to say about this?

- 1 Samuel 16:7: "But the LORD said to Samuel, "Do not look at his appearance or at the height of his stature, because I have refused him. For the Lord does not see as man sees; for man looks at the outward appearance, but the LORD looks at the heart" (NKJV).
- Jeremiah 17:9–10: "The heart is more deceitful than all else and is desperately sick; who can understand it? I, the LORD, search the heart, I test the mind, even to give to each man according to his ways, According to the results of his deeds" (NASB).
- Jeremiah 17:9–10: "The human heart is most deceitful and desperately wicked. Who really knows how bad it is? But I know! I, the LORD, search all hearts and examine secret motives. I give all people their due rewards,

according to what their actions deserve" (NLT). You see, we don't want a human heart that is deceitful, we need to ask God Almighty to change that human heart that is deceitful into a pure heart or a merry heart that does good like a medicine, a discerning heart.

- Psalm 24:3–4: "Who may ascend into the hill of the LORD? Or who may stand in His holy place? He who has clean hands and a pure heart, who has not lifted up his soul to an idol, nor sworn deceitfully" (NKJV).
- In Psalm 51:10, King David asked God to create in him a clean heart; a pure heart: "Create in me a clean heart, O God, and renew a steadfast spirit within me."
- First Timothy 1:5 says that "the purpose of my instruction is that all the Christians there would be filled with love that comes from a pure heart, a clear conscience, and sincere faith" (NLT).
- 2 Timothy 2:22: "Now flee from youthful lusts, (NLT says "Run from anything that stimulates youthful lust. Follow anything that makes you want to do right.) And pursue righteousness, faith, love and peace, with those who call on the Lord from a pure heart" (NASB).
- First Peter 1:22 says "to love one another fervently with a pure heart." The NLT says "So see to it that you really do love each other intensely with all your hearts."
- In Psalm 19:13, King David asked God that the words of his mouth and the meditation of his heart be acceptable: "May the words of my mouth and the thoughts of my heart be pleasing to you, O LORD, my rock and my redeemer" (NLT).
- Proverbs 17:20: "He who has a deceitful heart finds no good, The crooked heart will not prosper;" but in Proverbs 17:22, the writer of this Proverb tells us that "A merry heart does good, like medicine, But a broken spirit dries the bones." (NLT).
- Ecclesiastes 8:5: "He who keeps his command will experience nothing harmful; And a wise man's heart discerns both time and judgment."
- Jesus tells us in the Sermon on the Mount in Matthew 5:8: "God blesses those whose hearts are pure, for they will see God" (NLT).

Like David in Psalm 57:7 and also in Psalm 108:1, we should desire to have a steadfast or confident heart:

- "My heart is steadfast, O God, my heart is steadfast; I will sing and give praise. (Psalm 57:7) or the NLT calls it a confident heart-"My heart is confident in you, O God; no wonder I can sing your praises!"
- "O God, my heart is steadfast; I will sing and give praise, even with my glory. (Psalm 108:1) "My heart is confident in you, O God; no wonder I can sing your praises! Wake up, my soul" (NLT)!
- Psalm 112:7–8 tells us to have not only a steadfast or confident heart but also that our hearts should be established—"He will not be afraid of evil tidings; His heart is steadfast, trusting in the LORD. His heart is established; He will not be afraid, until he sees his desire upon his enemies."
- Proverbs 27:19 tells us that a man's heart reveals the man "As in water face reflects face, so a man's heart reveals the man."

The condition of a person's heart tells us much about that person-it shows us what that person is really like.

A Proud Heart

The Bible talks about how the human heart is proud or arrogant:

- Psalm 101:5: "Whoever secretly slanders his neighbor, him I will destroy; No one who has a haughty look and an arrogant heart will I endure." Or NLT says it this way "I will not tolerate people who slander their neighbors. I will not endure conceit and pride."
- Proverbs 21:4: "Haughty eyes, a proud heart, and evil actions are all sin" (NLT).
- Proverbs 28:25:" He who is of a proud heart stirs up strife, but he who trusts in the LORD will be prospered."
- Proverbs 16:5: "Everyone who is proud in heart is an abomination to the LORD; assuredly, he will not be unpunished" (NASB).
- Proverbs 18:12: "Before destruction the heart of a man is haughty, and before honor is humility." Or NLT puts it this way "Haughtiness goes before destruction; humility precedes honor."
- Proverbs 21:4: "Haughty eyes, a proud heart, and evil actions are all sin" (NLT).

- Proverbs 28:25–26: "He who is of a proud heart stirs up strife, but he who trusts in the LORD will be prospered. He who trusts in his own heart is a fool, but whoever walks wisely will be delivered."

God does not want us to have a proud heart; he wants us to have a humble heart.

- Jesus said in Matthew 11:29–30: "Take My yoke upon you, and learn from me, for I am gentle and humble in heart; and YOU SHALL FIND REST FOR YOUR SOULS. For My yoke is easy, and my load is light" (NASB).
- Colossians 3:12–15: "And so, as those who have been chosen of God, holy and beloved, put on a heart of compassion, kindness, humility, gentleness and patience; bearing with one another, and forgiving each other, whoever has a complaint against anyone; just as the Lord forgave you, so also should you. And beyond all these things put on love, which is the perfect bond of unity. And let the peace of Christ rule in your hearts, to which indeed you were called in one body; and be thankful" (NASB).

A Troubled Heart

The Bible refers to the human heart as a troubled heart and God tells us in His Word to not let our hearts be troubled. God has a plan, a purpose and a destiny for each and every one of us. You were not born by accident; you were born just when and where God wanted you to be born! The word *Troubled* in the following verses means: bothered, sad-low countenance, grieved, misfortune, heavy hearted, and broken.

- Jeremiah 1:5: "Before I formed you in the womb I knew you; before you were born I sanctified you; I ordained you a prophet to the nations."
- Jeremiah 29:11–13: "For I know the plans I have for you," says the LORD. "They are plans for good and not for disaster, to give you a future and a hope. In those days when you pray, I will listen. If you look for me in earnest, you will find me when you seek me" (NIV).
- 1 Samuel 24:5: "Now it happened afterward that David's heart troubled him because he had cut Saul's robe."
- 2 Samuel 4:1: "When Saul's son heard that Abner had died in Hebron, he lost heart, and all Israel was troubled."

- Job 4:5: "but now it comes upon you, and you are weary; it touches you, and you are troubled." The NIV says, "But now trouble comes to you, and you are discouraged; it strikes you, and you are dismayed."

- Psalms 6:2–19: "Have mercy on me, O LORD, for I am weak; O LORD, heal me, for my bones are troubled. My soul also is greatly troubled; But You, O LORD; how long? Return, O LORD, deliver me! Oh, save me for your mercies' sake! For in death there is no remembrance of you; In the grave who will give You thanks? I am weary with my groaning; all night I make my bed swim; I drench my couch with my tears. My eye wastes away because of grief; It grows old because of all my enemies. Depart from me, all you workers of iniquity; for the LORD has heard the voice of my weeping. The LORD has heard my supplication; The LORD will receive my prayer. Let all my enemies be ashamed and greatly troubled; let them turn back and be ashamed suddenly."

- Psalms 30:7: "LORD, by your favor you have made my mountain stand strong; you hid your face, and I was troubled. The NLT says, "Your favor, O LORD, made me as secure as a mountain. Then you turned away from me, and I was shattered."

- Psalms 38:6: "I am troubled, I am bowed down greatly; I go mourning all the day long. The NLT says, "I am bent over and racked with pain. My days are filled with grief."

- Psalms 77:4: "You hold my eyelids open; I am so troubled that I cannot speak." The NLT says, "You don't let me sleep. I am too distressed even to pray!"

- Lamentations 1:20: "See, O LORD, that I am in distress; my soul is troubled; my heart is overturned within me, for I have been very rebellious. Outside the sword bereaves, at home it is like death."

- Lamentations 2:11:"I have cried until the tears no longer come. My heart is broken (troubled in the KJV), my spirit poured out, as I see what has happened to my people. Little children and tiny babies are fainting and dying in the streets."

- Daniel 2:1: "Now in the second year of Nebuchadnezzar's reign, Nebuchadnezzar had dreams; and his spirit was so troubled that his sleep left him."

- Matthew 14:26: "and when the disciples saw Him walking on the sea, they were troubled, saying, 'It is a ghost!' And they cried out for fear."

Even Jesus had a troubled heart from time to time during His three short years of public ministry from the age of 30–33, or He addressed the issue of those he loved and cared about that had a troubled heart! *Troubled* here in these verses refers to a sorrowful spirit, a heavy heart; a grieving heart.

- Matthew 24:6: "And you will hear of wars and rumors of wars. See that you are not troubled; for all these things must come to pass, but the end is not yet."
- Mark 13:7: "But when you hear of wars and rumors of wars, do not be troubled; for such things must happen, but the end is not yet"
- Mark 14:33–34: "And He took Peter, James, and John with Him, and He began to be troubled and deeply distressed. Then He said to them, 'My soul is exceedingly sorrowful, even to death. Stay here and watch.'"
- Luke 10:41: "And Jesus answered and said to her, "Martha, Martha, you are worried and troubled about many things." The NIV says, "Martha, Martha," the Lord answered, "you are worried and upset about many things,"
- Luke 24:38 "And He said to them, 'Why are you troubled? And why do doubts arise in your hearts?'" The NLT says, "Why are you frightened?" he asked. "Why do you doubt who I am?"
- John 11:32–35: "Then, when Mary came where Jesus was, and saw Him, she fell down at His feet, saying to Him, 'Lord, if You had been here, my brother would not have died.' Therefore, when Jesus saw her weeping, and the Jews who came with her weeping, He groaned in the spirit and was troubled. And He said, 'Where have you laid him?' They said to Him, 'Lord, come and see.' Jesus wept."
- John 12:27–28a: "Now my soul is deeply troubled. Should I pray, 'Father, save me from what lies ahead'? But that is the very reason why I came! Father, bring glory to your name" (NLT).
- John 12:21: "When Jesus had said these things, He was troubled in spirit, and testified and said, 'Most assuredly, I say to you, one of you will betray me.'"
- John 14:1–4: "Let not your heart be troubled; you believe in God, believe also in Me. In My Father's house are many mansions; if it were not so, I would have told you. I go to prepare a place for you. And if I go and prepare a place for you, I will come again and receive you to myself; that where I am, there you may be also."

- John 14:27: "Peace I leave with you, my peace I give to you; not as the world gives do I give to you. Let not your heart be troubled, neither let it be afraid."

It is difficult for us to enter into the presence of the Lord if we have a troubled heart or spirit.

A Compassionate Heart

Jesus our Lord and Savior and the one whom we are to emulate had a heart of compassion. So we His disciples should have a heart of compassion also!

Webster's definition of *compassion* is: 1.) To feel pity; 2.) Sorrow for the sufferings or trouble of another or others, with the urge to help; 3.) Sympathy.

What does the Word of God have to say about compassion or a compassionate heart?

- Exodus 33:19: "Then He said, 'I will make all my goodness pass before you, and I will proclaim the name of the LORD before you. I will be gracious to whom I will be gracious, and I will have compassion on whom I will have compassion.'"
- Psalm 78:37–38: "For their heart was not steadfast toward Him, nor were they faithful in His covenant. But He, being compassionate, forgave their iniquity, and did not destroy them; and often He restrained His anger, and did not arouse all His wrath" (NASB).
- Psalm 86:15: "But You, O Lord, are a God full of compassion, and gracious, Longsuffering and abundant in mercy and truth."
- Psalm 145:8: "The LORD is gracious and full of compassion, Slow to anger and great in mercy."
- Matthew 14:14: "And when Jesus went out He saw a great multitude; and He was moved with compassion for them, and healed their sick."
- Matthew 20:34: "And moved with compassion, Jesus touched their eyes; and immediately they regained their sight and followed Him" (NASB).
- Mark 6:34: "And Jesus, when He came out, saw a great multitude and was moved with compassion for them, because they were like sheep not having a shepherd. So He began to teach them many things."

- 1 Peter 3: 8–9: "Finally, all of you be of one mind, having compassion for one another; love as brothers, be tenderhearted, be courteous; not returning evil for evil or reviling for reviling, but on the contrary blessing, knowing that you were called to this, that you may inherit a blessing."

Our Lord is looking for people who have a compassionate and passionate heart just like He had. The presence of the Lord will be with those who follow in His footsteps. We definitely need the presence of the Lord God Almighty in our lives each and every day or as much as possible.

Conclusion

I believe God Almighty reveals His glory to us daily through His creation and there are many spectacular places and natural landmarks that show us His creativity in this country and in many other countries too. Scripture reveals that this planet earth displays the awesome handiwork of our Lord! Nature in general, along with our own physical bodies, reveals the glory of an Almighty Maker or Creator. Our own bodies are the temple or tabernacle of God where the Lord has taken up residence in our hearts. The condition of our heart is very important to God. We have discussed the various heart conditions that are pleasing and not pleasing to God Almighty, that help us to enter into His presence or hinder us from entering into His presence. The Word of God tells us about these conditions extensively. In order for us to see the glory or presence of the Lord in our lives, we must have a pure heart and a compassionate heart! We must guard our hearts and minds. It is our responsibility to fill them with the Truth—God's holy word.

Chapter Two

Review Questions

1. Do you think God reveals His glory to us through His creation? If so how? Give a few examples and at least two Scripture references to back up your answer:

2. Which of our natural landmarks in this country demonstrate the glory of the Lord? Give at least three of them:
    1.)
    2.)
    3.)

3. Does the planet earth display the awesome handiwork of the Lord? Give two Scripture references to support your answer:
    1.)
    2.)

4. Do you believe that we can see the glory and wonder of our Lord in our own bodies? If so how? Give a couple of Scripture references to support your answer:

5. Is your body the temple of the Holy Spirit? Give two Scriptures that tell us that it is:

6. Is the condition of your heart important? If so, give some Bible verses that talk about the condition of our hearts:

7. What kind of heart did David say we should have in Psalms 57:7 and 108:1?

8. Where in the Bible does it talk about how the human heart is arrogant or prideful? Give at least 3 or 4 references:

    1.)

    2.)

    3.)

    4.)

9. If God does not want us to have a proud heart then what kind of heart does he want us to have?

10. The Word of God refers to the human heart as a _____ heart and God tells us in His Word to _____.

11. What does this word troubled mean in these verses? Also give a few Scripture references which speak about the troubled heart:

12. Even our Lord and Savior Jesus Christ had a troubled heart from time to time during his three years of public ministry. How did Jesus have a troubled heart? Give your definition of troubled in these verses! Give two examples in the Word of God when Jesus had this kind of troubled heart:

13. Jesus our Lord and Savior and the one whom we are to emulate had a heart of _____. Define this kind of heart? Do you have this kind of heart?

14. Write out and perhaps memorize at least one of three Scriptures that talk about a compassionate heart:

    1.)

    2.)

    3.)

CHAPTER THREE

How Do We Enter Into His Presence?

Review of Chapter Two

In chapter two, we discussed extensively how the glory of the Lord appears to us in many spectacular ways through what He has created. Do you see the glory of the Lord in His creation and the things He made for us to enjoy? Even our own bodies which are the temple or tabernacle of the Lord demonstrate the glory of an Almighty God. We talked about the various conditions of the heart and how that can help or hinder us from entering into His presence. We discussed the meaning of compassion and how important it is for us to have a heart of compassion like our Lord Jesus Christ had. Do not forget Psalm 24:3–4 where the writer David talks about who can ascend into the hill of the Lord and who may stand in His holy place? Only those whose hands and hearts are pure, who do not worship idols and never tell lies will be allowed to enter into His presence!

Step One: Repentance

Sin cannot enter into the presence of God. Before we can even begin to enter into His presence through the gate we have to repent-ask God to forgive us for our sins. We need to have clean hands and pure hearts before we can come before His throne room.

First, we need to examine our hearts to see if there is any sin there. I have read 1 John 1:9 many times and thought I knew what this verse of Scripture was saying but I didn't. God has revealed to me that we need to confess our sins, but we need to be specific about what those sins are. When we confess our sins to the Lord, we need to ask forgiveness for whatever sin it is we have committed. For example, if you have committed the sin of adultery this week, then you need to ask God to forgive you for that sin. You say God forgive me for committing adultery and with your help I promise not to do that any more. If you have told a lie today you need to go to your heavenly Father and say Father I told a lie I am sorry, please forgive me for lying and with your help I promise not to lie anymore. If you have stolen something this week then you need to tell your heavenly Father I stole money from my dad or mom and I am sorry. Please forgive me and with your help I promise not to steal anymore. If you have used God's name in vain recently, you need to confess that sin and ask God to forgive you and with His help you promise not to do that anymore.

Asking for forgiveness for our sins involves true repentance. True repentance means we not only confess our sins but we stop committing that sin and with the Lord's help—refuse to keep doing that which we know we are not supposed to do anymore. It is more than just being sorry for something wrong you did simply because you got caught at doing it. So before we can even attempt to enter into the presence of God we have to have clean hands and a pure heart. Sin cannot enter into the presence of God. David asked God in Psalm 51:3: "Create in me a clean heart, O God. Renew a right spirit within me." We need to ask God to do the same for us. God create in me a clean heart and renew a right spirit within me. May my hands be clean of all sin and may my heart be pure. Help me Lord to live a holy life.

God is a holy God and His standard for our way of living is to walk in holiness. If we want to be in God's presence, we need to live a life of holiness before God and others. We need to get rid of any sin in our lives and clothe ourselves with the Lord Jesus Christ. We cannot come into the presence of God with any kind of sin in our lives.

Step Two: Thanksgiving and Praise

Thanksgiving

The Bible tells us that we begin to enter into His presence with praise and thanksgiving. Psalm 100:4: "Enter his gates with thanksgiving; go into his courts with praise. Give thanks to him and bless his name" (NLT). Praise is only the beginning of our entering into His presence. The Bible tells us here that we enter into his gates or presence with thanksgiving and praise. Praise is the means into which we enter into His presence. We just begin to enter into His presence with praise. There is more to it than that. Don't stop there. Go on farther! The late Ruth

Ward Heflin in her book called *Glory* admonishes us to "praise until the spirit of worship comes. Worship until the glory comes. Then we are to stand in the glory!" Praise is just the first step in entering into His presence. We need to pray the power or glory down from heaven.

As a child, I grew up on a farm 5 miles from the big town of George, Iowa. I lived there the first 18 years of my life. I was a country girl. I remember we had a gate that went from the farmyard out to the pasture. The gate was the entry way into the pasture and creek where the cattle grazed. It also kept the cattle out of the yard and in the pasture.

Some of you who have a fenced in yard have a gate into your yard. That gate serves as the entry way into your yard. Likewise, praise is the entry way into the presence of the Lord. Just as the gate only allows entry into and out of the pasture or yard, praise allows us to enter into His presence.

King David had much to say about praising the Lord and the power of praise. We need to praise God from our hearts. We have so much to praise Him for. Instead of thinking about what you don't have, try thinking and praising God for what you do have. My mother taught me at a young age to be thankful and appreciative for those things the Lord has blessed me with, and that I was not to expect God to give me more when I didn't appreciate what I already have. Our blessings are much more than just material things or stuff! David says in Psalm 34:1:"I will bless the LORD at all times; His praise shall continually be in my mouth." We should be praising God continually. If we are doing that, we will not have time to grumble and complain like we often do. Murmuring, complaining, fault-finding, back-biting, and being so picky about every little thing will not help you develop a lifestyle of praise and worship unto the Lord. So next time you sit down to eat or go out to eat instead of finding something wrong with the food or not liking it why don't you praise God that you have food to eat.

Not long ago, Seth and I, along with a group of other people from our church, went to Haiti to visit our daughter who was working there as a missionary. Many times the people there go without food for several days at a time. One man told us he only eats once in three days so that his family and others he knows could eat. He shares his food with others. They come up to you there and rub their stomachs and tell you they are hungry.

Shortly before we had gotten to Haiti, Michelle told us how she and Bette saw a woman in church with this little baby, named Daisy. Michelle asked the lady if she could hold the baby and Michelle said the baby was so weak it couldn't even lift her little head up. She was almost dead from starvation. Michelle also said she cried for an hour or more when she first held that precious little baby in her arms. They found out later that the baby was not this lady's, but the mother had given her the baby because the baby was sick and she was unable to care for her. The woman who took the baby had five children of her own so she was not able to take care of her adequately and give her the milk she needed. So after much prayer, Michelle and Bette went to the woman who was taking care of Daisy and asked her if they could have the baby. I saw the baby a few days after Betty and Michelle got the baby. Her arms were drawn up and she looked so frail and undernourished. My heart went out to her. Daisy was three months old or maybe even older and she only weighed five to six pounds. When I saw her after she had been given some milk, she was smiling and lifting her head. We found out later after taking her to the doctor that she had spinal meningitis along with some other physical needs. After much prayer, fasting, and believing, God miraculously healed her. With the Lord's help Michelle loved and cared for that baby for over a month and was able to put her in an orphanage in Port-au-Prince where she was adopted by a Christian couple in Michigan.

Many people in Haiti and other parts of the world are faced with these kinds of heartbreaking problems in their lives every day. They go hungry, thirsty, and have no food, clothing, or a place to live. We are a blessed people and the nation of United States of America is a blessed nation. As God's children, we should be the most blessed (happy) people in the whole world and we should always praise Him and thank Him for what we have, what He has done for us, in us and through us. We serve a great and mighty God and He is worthy of our praise. He alone is worthy to receive glory and honor and praise. So then why do we murmur and complain so much?

- In John 6:43 Jesus tells us to "Stop grumbling among yourselves" (NIV). That's a command—grumbling and complaining will not get us into God's presence, that's for sure.
- Philippians 2:14–15: "Do all things without grumbling or disputing; that you may prove yourselves to be blameless and innocent, children of God above

reproach in the midst of a crooked and perverse generation, among whom you appear as lights in the world" (NASB).

When Seth and I first got married in 1970, I remember many times standing at the sink and praising God for running water. To be able to just turn on a faucet and for water to come out was a real blessing to me. Seth found this to be a little strange and unusual and asked me what I was doing. I told him I was praising the Lord that I no longer had to carry water, but could just turn on a faucet and there it was. You see, growing up on the farm we had to carry our water in five gallon buckets up to the house which was about a block away from the pump or well. Boy, did I dislike wash day! That meant I had to haul all that water up to the house so mom could wash clothes. That was never a pleasant experience especially in the wintertime when it was so cold. I must admit it built character and strength in me. In the long run it was good for me.

Too many times we take the little things for granted and forget to thank God for them. Little insignificant things—details are important to God and should be important to us also. For example, take our bodies, our health, our minds, how many of us thank God for a strong, healthy body and a sound mind every single day. We need to start thanking God for the simple things in life. We need to thank Him for food on our table, clothes on our backs, and a roof over our head instead of complaining about the food that we don't like it or it isn't cooked just right, or our clothes are old and tattered or out of style, or our house is too small, too old, or whatever. We should be praising God all the time. We have much to praise and worship God for and about in this country—the United States of America. Let your lips offer up to God a sacrifice of praise at all times. His praise shall continually be on our lips. Let the fruit of your mouth be praise and worship unto God your Creator and Provider. Psalm 34:1 says "I will bless the LORD at all times; His praise shall continually be in my mouth."

Like I said before, King David had much to say about praise in the book of Psalms. Here are just a few verses from Psalms that speak about giving our praise unto the Lord:

- Psalm 9:1–2: "I will praise You, O LORD, with my whole heart; I will tell of all your marvelous works. I will be glad and rejoice in you; I will sing praise to your name, O Most High."

- Psalm 35:28: "And my tongue shall speak of your righteousness and of Your praise all the day long."
- Psalm 63:3–5: "Your unfailing love is better to me than life itself; how I praise you! I will honor you as long as I live, lifting up my hands to you in prayer. You satisfy me more than the richest of foods. I will praise you with songs of joy" (NLT).
- Psalm 69:30: "I will praise the name of God with a song, and will magnify Him with thanksgiving."
- Psalm 71:6–8: "By You I have been upheld from birth; you are He who took me out of my mother's womb. My praise shall be continually of you. Let my mouth be filled with your praise and with your glory all the day."
- Psalm 86:12: "I will praise You, O Lord my God, with all my heart, and I will glorify your name forevermore."
- Psalm 99:3: "Let them praise your great and awesome name; He is holy."
- Psalm 100:4: "Enter into His gates with thanksgiving, And into His courts with praise. Be thankful to Him, and bless His name."
- Psalm 104:33: "I will sing to the LORD all my life; I will sing praise to my God as long as I live" (NIV).
- Psalm 106:1: "Praise the LORD! Give thanks to the LORD, for he is good! His faithful love endures forever" (NLT).
- Psalm 106:48–107:1: "Blessed be the LORD, the God of Israel, from everlasting to everlasting! Let all the people say, 'Amen!' Praise the LORD! Give thanks to the LORD, for he is good! His faithful love endures forever" (NLT).
- Psalm 109:30: "But I will give repeated thanks to the LORD, praising him to everyone" (NLT).
- Psalm 113:1–3: "Praise the LORD! Praise, O servants of the LORD, Praise the name of the LORD! Blessed be the name of the LORD From this time forth and forevermore! From the rising of the sun to its going down The Lord's name is to be praised."
- Psalm 115:18: "But we will bless the LORD From this time forth and forevermore. Praise the LORD!"
- Psalm 118:21: "I thank you for answering my prayer and saving me" (NLT)!
- Psalm 118:28: "You are my God, and I will praise you; you are my God, I will exalt you."

- Psalm 135:1–3: "Praise the LORD! Praise the name of the LORD! Praise him, you who serve the LORD, you who serve in the house of the LORD, in the courts of the house of our God. Praise the LORD, for the LORD is good; celebrate his wonderful name with music" (NLT).
- Psalm 145:2–3: "Every day I will bless you, and I will praise your name forever and ever. Great is the LORD, and greatly to be praised;"
- Psalm 145:10: "All Your works shall praise You, O LORD, and your saints shall bless you."
- Psalm 146:2: "While I live I will praise the LORD; I will sing praises to my God while I have my being."
- Psalm 147:1: "Praise the LORD! For it is good to sing praises to our God; for it is pleasant, and praise is beautiful."
- Psalm 149:1: "Praise the LORD! Sing to the LORD a new song, And His praise in the assembly of saints."
- Psalm 149:3: "Let them praise His name with the dance; Let them sing praises to Him with the timbrel and harp."
- Psalm 150:1–6: "Praise the LORD! Praise God in His sanctuary; Praise Him in His mighty firmament! Praise Him for His mighty acts; Praise Him according to His excellent greatness! Praise Him with the sound of the trumpet; Praise Him with the lute and harp! Praise Him with the timbrel and dance; Praise Him with stringed instruments and flutes! Praise Him with loud cymbals; Praise Him with clashing cymbals! Let everything that has breath praise the LORD. Praise the LORD!"

Praise

We can see from these Scripture verses in the book of Psalms that we come into His presence with thanksgiving and praise. So the next step in how to enter into His presence is praise.

In the New Testament from the Message Bible, John says in John 10:7–11 that Jesus is the gate for the sheep. All those others are up to no good—sheep stealers, every one of them. But the sheep didn't listen to them. I am the gate. Anyone who goes through me will be cared for—will freely go in and out and find pasture. We can freely go in and out of the presence of God through the gate. A thief is only there to steal and kill and to destroy. The enemy tries to keep us from entering the gate. He doesn't want us to enter into the presence of the Lord. He does whatever it takes to distract us and get our minds on other things while we are trying to enter into the presence of the Lord. So we need to keep our minds stayed on the Lord—focus on Him. Praise Him, rejoice in Him. He needs to be our focal point as we enter into His presence. Forget about everyone and everything else around you and concentrate and meditate only on Jesus and His great love for you. Jesus said in John 10:10 that he came so that we could have real and eternal life, more and better life than we ever dreamed of. Jesus is the gate! Enter into His presence through the gate. The Bible tells us to enter into His presence with praise and thanksgiving.

Step Three: Worship

After we have entered into His presence by thanking and praising Him, we need to press on in and begin to worship Him. God wants us to praise Him until the spirit of worship comes upon us. If our objective is to live in the presence of God or the glory realm, then we need to be true worshipers. We need to spend more time worshiping Him. Jesus told the Samaritan woman at the well in John 4:22–24: "You Samaritans know so little about the one you worship, while we Jews know all about him, for salvation comes through the Jews. But the time is coming and is already here when true worshipers will worship the Father in spirit and in truth. The Father is looking for anyone who will worship him that way. For God is Spirit, so those who worship him must worship in spirit and in truth" (NLT).

God is looking for true worshipers who will worship Him in spirit and in truth. God is seeking us to worship Him. True worship comes from our hearts, out of our spirits, in love and adoration unto the Lord. Are you a true worshiper or do you want to be?

Definition of Worship

Webster defines worship as:
1. Extreme devotion, intense love or admiration of any kind,
2. Greatness of character; honor; dignity; worthiness;
3. To show religious devotion or reverence for;
4. Adore, or venerate as a deity;
5. Idolize; revere, adore-adoration

The Hebrew word for worship is *Shachah*, which means to:

1. Bow (self) down, crouch, fall down (flat), humbly
2. Beseech, do (make) obeisance, do reverence, make to stoop, worship.

What the Bible Says about Worship

The Bible also has much to say about worship because worship ushers us into the presence of God:

- Exodus 34:14: "Do not worship any other god, for the LORD, whose name is Jealous, is a jealous God" (NIV).
- Psalms 22:27–28: "All the ends of the world shall remember and turn to the LORD, and all the families of the nations shall worship before you. For the kingdom is the Lord's, And He rules over the nations."
- Psalm 29:2: "Give unto the LORD the glory due to His name; Worship the LORD in the beauty of holiness."
- Psalm 66:4: "Everything on earth will worship you; they will sing your praises, shouting your name in glorious songs" (NLT).
- Psalm 95:6: "Oh come, let us worship and bow down; Let us kneel before the LORD our Maker."
- Psalm 96:9: "Worship the LORD in his entire holy splendor. Let all the earth tremble before him" (NLT).
- Psalm 138:2: "I will worship toward your holy temple, and praise your name For Your loving-kindness and your truth; for you have magnified your word above all your name."
- Isaiah 66:23: "All humanity will come to worship me from week to week and from month to month" (NLT).
- Zephaniah 2:11: "The LORD will be awesome to them when he destroys all the gods of the land. The nations on every shore will worship him, every one in its own land" (NLT).
- Matthew 4:9–10: "And he said to Him, "All these things I will give you if you will fall down and worship me." Then Jesus said to him, "Away with you, Satan! For it is written, 'You shall worship the LORD your God, and Him only you shall serve.'"
- John 4:20–24: "Our fathers worshiped on this mountain and you Jews say that in Jerusalem is the place where one ought to worship. Jesus said to her,

'Woman, believe me, the hour is coming when you will neither on this mountain, nor in Jerusalem, worship the Father. You worship what you do not know; we know what we worship, for salvation is of the Jews. But the hour is coming, and now is, when the true worshipers will worship the Father in spirit and truth; for the Father is seeking such to worship Him. God is Spirit and those who worship Him must worship in spirit and truth.'"

- Revelation 4:9–11: "Whenever the living creatures give glory and honor and thanks to Him who sits on the throne, who lives forever and ever, the twenty-four elders fall down before Him who sits on the throne and worship Him who lives forever and ever, and cast their crowns before the throne, saying: "You are worthy, O Lord, To receive glory and honor and power; For You created all things, And by Your will they exist and were created."

- Revelation 14:6–7: "Then I saw another angel flying in midair, and he had the eternal gospel to proclaim to those who live on the earth—to every nation, tribe, language and people. He said in a loud voice, "Fear God and give him glory, because the hour of his judgment has come. Worship him who made the heavens, the earth, the sea and the springs of water" (NIV).

- Revelation 15:4: "Who will not fear you, O Lord, and bring glory to your name? For you alone are holy. All nations will come and worship before you, for your righteous acts have been revealed" (NIV).

- Revelation 19:10: "Then I fell down at his feet to worship him, but he said, 'No, don't worship me. For I am a servant of God, just like you and other believers who testify of their faith in Jesus. Worship God. For the essence of prophecy is to give a clear witness for Jesus'" (NLT).

- Revelation 22:8–9: "I, John, am the one who saw and heard all these things. And when I saw and heard these things, I fell down to worship the angel who showed them to me. But again he said, "No, don't worship me. I am a servant of God, just like you and your brothers the prophets, as well as all who obey what is written in this scroll. Worship God" (NLT)!

God's power will be revealed to us in signs and wonders, miracles of healings, salvation of the lost, and seeing the captives set free from all bondages, when we truly get into His presence through our praise and worship with all our hearts and minds. Praise and worship will catapult us into the presence of the Lord. We will begin to see an awesome move of God in all His glory, might, and power as we give ourselves in praise and worship to Him and Him alone.

We need to all be in one accord, in unity and harmony in the body of Christ like the New Testament saints. We will be ushered into the presence of the Lord when we with one voice give our sacrifice of praise and worship unto an awesome, mighty, and powerful Father. Bring your sacrifice of praise and worship to God as a sweet-smelling fragrance to Him.

Our goal or purpose in praising and worshiping Him should be to enter into His presence each and every time! Oh, how our heavenly Father loves to hear our praise and worship to Him. There is power and freedom in praise and worship. Oh, that we would understand and get hold of that power! Help us Lord to know the power of praise and worship!

The Seven Pillars to Worship

In 2012, I went to Kidfest with a group from our denomination which is the Church of God Cleveland, Tennessee. Over 2,500 children and chaperones attended this event. On Sunday morning there was an awesome outpouring of the Holy Spirit upon our young people, the man speaking taught on these seven pillars to worship which I am going to share in this book. These Hebrew words for praise can be found on the internet.

Pillar 1: Halal

- A primary Hebrew root word for praise.
- Our word *hallelujah* comes from this base word.
- It means "to shine, to boast, show, to rave, celebrate, to be clamorously foolish, to dance."

Scriptures where praise is interpreted as *halal:*

- Psalm 113:1–3: "Praise *(halal)* ye the LORD. Praise (halal), O ye servants of the LORD, praise *(halal)* the name of the LORD" (KJV).
- Psalm 150: 1: "Praise *(halal)* the LORD! Praise (halal) God in His sanctuary; Praise *(halal)* Him in His mighty expanse" (NASB).
- Psalm 149:3: "Let them praise *(halal)* his name in the dance: let them sing praises unto him with the timbrel and harp" (KJV).

Pillar 2: Yadah

- *Yadah* is a verb with a root meaning, the extended hand, to throw out the hand, therefore to worship with extended hand.
- The lifting up of the hands.

Scripture verses that use *yadah:*

- 2 Chronicles 20:21: "And when he had consulted with the people, he appointed those who sang to the LORD and those who praised Him in holy attire, as they went out before the army and said, 'Give thanks (*yadah*) to the LORD, for His loving kindness is everlasting'" (NASB).
- Psalm 63:4: "So I will bless Thee as long as I live; I will (*yadah*) lift up my hands in Thy name" (NASB).
- Psalm 107:15: "Oh that men would praise (*yadah*) the LORD for his goodness, and for his wonderful works to the children of men!" (KJV).

Pillar 3: Towdah

- Comes from the same principle root word as yadah, but is used more specifically.
- *Towdah* literally means, "an extension of the hand in adoration, avowal, and acceptance. The giving of praise as a sacrifice!"
- In the Psalms and elsewhere it is used for thanking God for "things not received" as well as things already at hand.

Some Scriptures that contain *towdah* are:

- Psalm 50:14: "Offer to God a sacrifice of thanksgiving (*towdah*), And pay your vows to the Most High" (NASB).
- Psalm 50:23: "Whoso offereth praise (*towdah*) glorifieth me: and to him that ordereth his conversation aright will I show the salvation of God" (KJV).

Pillar 4: Shabach

- *Shabach* means, "to shout, to address in a loud tone, to command, to triumph."

Some Scriptures that use *shabach* are:

- Psalm 47:1: "Oh, clap your hands, all you peoples! Shout (*shabach*) to God with the voice of triumph!"
- Psalm 145:4: "One generation shall praise (*shabach*) Your works to another, And shall declare Your mighty acts."
- Isaiah 12:6: "Cry aloud and shout (*shabach*) for joy, O inhabitant of Zion, For great in your midst is the Holy One of Israel" (NASB).

Pillar 5: Barak

- *Barak* means to kneel down, to bless God as an act of adoration by bowing.

Some Scriptures that use *barak* are:

- Psalm 95:6: "O come, let us worship and bow down: let us kneel (*barak*) before the LORD our maker" (KJV).
- 2 Chronicles 29:20: "Then David said to all the assembly, "Now bless (*barak*) the LORD your God." And all the assembly blessed the LORD, the God of their fathers, and bowed low and did homage to the LORD and to the king" (NASB).
- Psalm 34:1: "I will bless (*barak*) the LORD at all times; His praise shall continually be in my mouth."

Pillar 6: Zamar

- *Zamar* means to pluck the strings of an instrument.
- To sing, to praise.
- A musical word which is largely involved with joyful expressions of music with musical instruments.

Some Scriptures that use *Zamar* are:

- Psalm 21:13: "Be thou exalted, LORD, in thine own strength: so will we sing and praise (zamar) thy power" (KJV).
- 1 Chronicles 16:9: "Sing to Him, sing praises (zamar) to Him; speak of all His wonders" (KJV).
- Psalm 57:8–9: "Awake, my glory; Awake, harp and lyre, I will awaken the dawn! I will give thanks to Thee, O Lord, among the peoples; I will sing praises (zamar) to Thee among the nations" (NASB).

- Psalm 150:1–5: "Praise the LORD! Praise God in His sanctuary; Praise Him in His mighty expanse. Praise Him for His mighty deeds; Praise Him according to His excellent greatness. Praise Him with trumpet sound; Praise Him with harp and lyre. Praise Him with timbrel and dancing; Praise Him with stringed instruments and pipe. Praise Him with loud cymbals; Praise Him with resounding cymbals. Let everything that has breath praise (zamar) the LORD. Praise the LORD" (NASB)!

Pillar 7: Tehillah

- *Tehillah* is devived from the word *halal.*
- It means "the singing of *halal,* to sing or laud
- Perceived to involve music, especially singing.
- Hymns of the Spirit.

Some Scriptures that use *tehillah* are:

- Psalm 22:3: "Yet Thou art holy, O Thou who art enthroned upon the praises (tehillah) of Israel" (NASB).
- Psalm 33:1: "Rejoice in the LORD, O you righteous! For praise (tehillah) from the upright is beautiful."
- Isaiah 61:3: "To grant those who mourn in Zion, Giving them a garland instead of ashes, The oil of gladness instead of mourning, The mantle of praise (tehillah) instead of a spirit of fainting. So they will be called oaks of righteousness, The planting of the LORD, that He may be glorified" (NASB).

Step Four: Living a Holy or Separated Life unto our Lord

The Word of God teaches us that unless we pursue peace and live a life of holiness we will not see God—we will not go to heaven and live with our heavenly Father and His Son forever. Hebrews 12:14 says, "Try to live in peace with everyone, and seek to live a clean and holy life, for those who are not holy will not see the Lord" (NLT). Our God is a holy God and no sin will enter into heaven. The Bible repeatedly encourages the believer to live a holy or separated life! The person who professes to be a child of a holy God should with the help of the Holy Spirit attempt to follow and be obedient to the principles and commands of the Word of God. This man or woman should live a life of integrity meaning that he or she adheres or follows a strict code of ethics which is based on the Word of God—the Bible! Now I know that no one can live a perfect, sinless life; that is why we have a mediator Jesus Christ our Lord the Son of God. But we should strive to live a life that pleases our heavenly Father and manifests our profession that we are believers.

In our church we call this process sanctification—living a life separated from this sinful world—not doing those things that we know to be contrary to the Word of God. We are in the world but not of this world. Jesus prayed for his disciples and we are His disciples. In John 17:16 Jesus said "They are not of the world, just as I am not of the world." He went on to say that we would be sanctified by the truth, which is the Word of God. Here are a couple other Scriptures that speak to the believer about separating ourselves from this evil sinful world and not acting and reacting the way they do. We should be different and set an example to those who are watching us to live a life of integrity! We should obey all the commands and advice of the Word of God. James tells us in James 1:22 to be "doers of the word, and not hearers only, deceiving yourselves."

- 2 Corinthians 6: 14–7:1 "Do not be unequally yoked together with unbelievers. For what fellowship has righteousness with lawlessness? And what communion has light with darkness? And what accord has Christ with Belial? Or what part has a believer with an unbeliever? And what agreement has the temple of God with idols? For you are the temple of the living God. As God has said: "I will dwell in them and walk among them. I will be their God, and they shall be My people." Therefore "Come out from among them and be separate, says the Lord. Do not touch what is unclean, and I will receive you." "I will be a Father to you, and you shall be My sons and daughters, says the LORD Almighty." Therefore, having these promises, beloved, let us cleanse ourselves from all filthiness of the flesh and spirit, perfecting holiness in the fear of God.
- 1 John 2:15–17: "Do not love the world or anything in the world. If anyone loves the world, the love of the Father is not in him. For everything in the world—the cravings of sinful man, the lust of his eyes and the boasting of what he has and does—comes not from the Father but from the world. The world and its desires pass away, but the man who does the will of God lives forever" (NIV).

- Psalm 24:3–5 "Who may ascend into the hill of the LORD? Or who may stand in His holy place? He who has clean hands and a pure heart, Who has not lifted up his soul to an idol, Nor sworn deceitfully. He shall receive blessing from the LORD, and righteousness from the God of his salvation."

King David in this Psalm tells us that those who have clean hands and a pure heart are the ones who can come into His presence. That happens in our daily personal devotions, but when we are in a corporate setting with other believers sometimes the presence or glory of the Lord comes down on the saint and sinner alike. Do you think living a life of holiness and integrity is necessary in order to experience the presence or glory of the Lord in your life? Why or why not?

Conclusion

This chapter was all about the steps we need to take biblically in order to enter into the presence of an Almighty God who is holy. Most importantly, sin can not enter into His presence, so the first step is to repent of any and all sin in our lives. Psalm 100:4 tells us that the second step to come into His presence is through thanksgiving and praise. After we have sincerely given Him thanks and praised Him for who He is and what He has done for us we need to press on until we begin to worship Him. In this chapter we also discussed the definition of worship and how in the Bible worship appears in several various forms and types. We worship as a body of Christ together in church or individually in our private devotions each day. After we have felt His presence by worshiping Him we should then continue to press on into the glory realm where the miracles of God are manifested and where we can abide! Lastly I shared with you the seven pillars or Hebrew words for praise in God's Word. We need to pray for God to help us have uninhibited praise like I see our children have! We also discussed the importance of living a holy life, a life of integrity and a life obedient to the commandments and guidelines of the Word of God. This truth is a necessity if we expect to experience the presence of the Lord in our daily lives. Yet in the body of Christ if you are present when this glory or presence falls down on His people as a sinner you too can sense or experience His presence!

Chapter Three

Review Questions

1. What is the first step to entering into the presence of the Lord?

2. What is the difference between just repenting and true repentance?

3. So before we can attempt to enter into the presence of a holy God we have to have _____ and a _____.

4. What did David ask God to do for him in Psalm 51:3?

5. What is step two for entering into His presence? Give a verse from the Bible to support your answer.

6. _____ had much to say about praising the Lord and the power of praise in the _____.

7. King David says in Psalm 34:1: "I will bless the Lord at _____ times; His praise shall _____ be in my mouth."

8. What is the antidote for a complaining spirit and is it a sin for us to grumble or complain? If so, write and memorize one Scripture to support your belief.

9. Write out at least three verses from David's book of Psalms which speak about giving our praise unto the Lord: Memorize at least one of them!

    1.)

    2.)

    3.)

10. The second step to entering into His presence involves thanksgiving and _____.

11. Is praise different from thanksgiving? If so, how?

12. Step three in this process of entering into His presence is what?

13. _____ worship comes from our hearts, out of our spirits, in love and adoration unto our Lord.

14. What is your definition of worship? How is it different from praise?

15. The Bible also has much to say about worship because worship ushers us in the presence of an Almighty God. Give at least four Scripture references about worship. Memorize at least one of them!

    1.)

    2.)

    3.)

    4.)

16. _____ will catapult us into the presence of an Almighty God.

17. Bring your sacrifice of praise and worship to God as a _____ to Him.

18. What should be our goal or purpose in praising and worshiping our Lord and King?

19. Do you believe there is power in praise and worship? If so, describe how that power is manifested:

20. Name the seven pillars or Hebrew words for praise and give a brief meaning of each and one Scripture verse that uses that word:

    1.)

    2.)

    3.)

    4.)

    5.)

    6.)

    7.)

21. We should pray and ask God to help us have _____ worship like our children have.

CHAPTER FOUR

Abiding or Staying in the Presence of God

Review of Chapter Three

In chapter three, we thoroughly discussed how we can get into the presence of an Almighty God. We talked about the various steps that are necessary to feel His presence and see His glory revealed to us. These steps are:

- Step One: Repentance
- Step Two: Thanksgiving and Praise
- Step Three: Worship
- Step Four: Living a Holy or Separated Life Unto our Lord

The goal of chapter three was to get us to understand the process we need to take in order to feel God's presence and to see His glory manifested in the body of Christ and in our lives! I also shared with you the seven pillars or Hebrew words for praise, their meaning and where they are found in the Bible. Now let's discover what it means to abide and stay in the presence of God.

What Does it Mean to Abide or Stay in His Presence?

What do I mean when I encourage you to abide or stay in the presence of the Lord? The word *abides* means:

- To stand fast; remain; go on being
- To stay; reside
- To await
- To submit to; put up with
- Continue, stay

Abiding means:

- Continuing without change
- Enduring
- Lasting

The word *stay* has many meanings, but the meaning of the word *stay* in regard to the presence of the Lord means:

- To linger; to tarry
- To strengthen, comfort, or sustain in mind and spirit
- Remain; never leave
- To pause; tarry; wait; delay
- To be able to continue or endure; hold out; last
- To stand still; stop; halt

So abiding or staying in the presence of God is a combination of all these meanings. Abiding involves someone who is able to endure or continue on even through great opposition!

John 8:31–32 says, "Then Jesus said to those Jews who believed Him, 'If you abide in my word, you are my disciples indeed. And you shall know the truth, and the truth shall make you free.'"

John 14:16–17 says, "And I will pray the Father, and He will give you another Helper, that He may abide with you forever; the Spirit of truth, whom the world cannot receive, because it neither sees Him nor knows Him; but you know Him, for He dwells with you and will be in you."

Step One: Praise and Worship the Lord Continually

Now that we know what it means to abide or stay in His presence, how do we accomplish this goal? This is by no means easy, but I believe it is attainable. How? The first step to accomplish this goal is to continually praise and worship the Lord. Day and night our lips should praise and worship him. King David says in Psalm 34:1: "I will bless the LORD at all times; His praise shall continually be in my mouth." Having an attitude of praise and worship all day long will help you abide or stay in the presence of God all the time. In every thing give thanks unto the Lord-not for but in! Even when things are not going your way for the moment or season in your life be thankful anyway, and especially when you don't feel like praising the Lord. Offer up the sacrifice of praise and worship at all times and in every situation or circumstance you find yourself in.

Do not let the enemy discourage you, depress or oppress you in any way. Do not let the enemy defeat you or over take you. Remember, greater is He who is in us than he who is in the world. The greater One—Jesus Christ lives big inside of you, and Satan and his demons have no power or authority over you. Jesus told his disciples in Luke 10:19: "Behold, I give you the authority to trample on serpents and scorpions, and over all the power of the enemy, and nothing shall by any means hurt you." We are over-comers by the blood of the lamb and the word of our testimony. Romans 8:37 tells us that we are more than conquerors through Him who loved us. Don't take any guff from the enemy-as soon as he tries to come into your home or life, kick him out-tell him he is not welcome in your house and in the name of Jesus to get out and stay out! Whenever the devil tries to come into my house and mess with me or my family, I go to the front door open it and with my foot I kick him out. I tell him to leave me and my household alone in the name of Jesus.

1 Samuel 30:6 says, "And David was greatly distressed; for the people spake of stoning him, because the soul of all the people was grieved, every man for his sons and for his daughters: but David encouraged himself in the LORD his God" (KJV). There was a time when King David was in serious trouble because his men were very bitter about losing their wives and children, and they began to talk of stoning him. But David found strength in the Lord his God and he had to encourage himself. When there is no one around to encourage you, then you will need to encourage yourself by reading and confessing what the Word of God says about you not what you feel or think at that moment when you are discouraged and down hearted. The Lord is the strength of our lives. Nehemiah tells us that the joy of the Lord is our strength. So don't let Satan steal your joy, because if he can steal your joy you will have no strength.

Step Two: Use Your Authority as a Believer

The second important Bible principle to remember is your authority as a believer. One of the great truths of Christ's redemptive work on the cross is the authority of the believer. Our Lord Jesus Christ clearly walked in authority during His earthly ministry. This authority was so clear and pronounced, that other people remarked about it and that distinguished Him from other religious leaders of that time. Christ demonstrated this authority as a model for all believers. In other words, He used this authority to show His followers the power which would be available to them after the resurrection. We must remember that Christ's authority has been given to the church—the body of Christ. Some believers are not aware of this and approach the problems of life as if they must submit to them. We are called not only to resist temptation, but all the works of the devil. We must not lose sight of the place of authority Christ has afforded us. We have authority in this earth, and we must use it to help us to abide in His presence!

As the body of Christ, we are seated in heavenly places with Christ Jesus-Satan is under our feet! The blood of Jesus is against you, Satan! You have no power or authority over us in the name of Jesus. We must realize that Satan is a defeated foe; he was defeated two thousand years ago when Jesus died on that cross for you and me! When Jesus defeated the enemy on the cross, He gave us authority over him. Jesus said in Luke 10:19: "Behold, I give you the authority to trample on serpents and scorpions, and over all the power of the enemy, and nothing shall by any means hurt you."

We are all involved in a spiritual battle with an enemy who will never give up or let us go. Just as God has a plan for you, so does the enemy of our souls! Satan's plan is to steal from you and destroy your life. "The thief does not come except to steal, and to kill, and to destroy" (John 10:10). He never takes a day off either. He is constantly trying to see his plan for your life come to pass. That is why we need to "be sober, be vigilant; because our adversary the devil prowls around like a roaring lion looking for someone to devour." Ask the Holy Spirit to help you discern the enemy's work in your life. Then "resist the devil and he will flee from you" (James 4:7).

The Weapons of Our Warfare

God has given us many weapons to use against the enemy's plan to destroy us, but here are the top seven weapons of our warfare to use against Satan.

Weapon One: Praise

The devil hates it each and every time we praise and worship God Almighty. When we praise and worship God, His presence dwells powerfully in our midst and the devil has to leave. He cannot and will not hang around where there is true worship. So become a true worshiper of God.

Weapon Two: Obedience:

If we are living in sin or walking in disobedience in any way, this leaves the door open for Satan to come into our lives and gain entry into our spirits and eventually a foothold. Satan does not have dominion over us, but disobedience to the Word of God or the Spirit of God opens the door for him to come in. Confession and repentance will smack the door in his face. The Bible tells us that obedience is better than sacrifice. (1 Samuel 15:22).

Weapon Three: God's Word

This is the most powerful weapon or tool of all. Jesus used the Word of God himself against the enemy when He was led into the wilderness by the Holy Spirit and Satan came to tempt Him. (Matthew 4:1–10). Each and every time the devil tried to tempt Jesus He used the Word of God to defeat him. Jesus said it is written and then he proceeded to quote the Word of God to Satan. Jesus used the Word of God to refute and rebuke the devil-when the devil tries to destroy your life or cause havoc in your life, refute and rebuke him with God's Word.

- Proverbs 27:12 says, "The prudent see danger and take refuge, but the simple keep going and suffer for it" (NIV). The very moment you see evil working in your life, hide yourself in the Word of God.
- David tells us in Psalm 119:11 to hide God's Word in our hearts so that we will not sin against him.
- Psalm 119:105 says, "The Word of God is a lamp to our feet and a light to our path."

The Word of God is living and powerful. Hebrews 4:12 says, "For the word of God is living and powerful, and sharper than any two-edged sword, piercing even to the division of soul and spirit, and of joints and marrow, and is a discerner of the thoughts and intents of the heart."

Weapon 4: Faith

- 1 Peter 5:8–9 says, "Be careful! Watch out for attacks from the Devil, your great enemy. He prowls around like a roaring lion, looking for some victim to devour. Take a firm stand against the enemy, and be strong in your faith. Remember that Christians all over the world are going through the same kind of suffering you are" (NLT). Peter tells us in these verses of Scripture to take a firm stand against our enemy and be strong in our faith.
- How do we remain strong in our faith? Romans 10:17 tells us we obtain faith by hearing and listening to the Word of God. Staying in the Word of God builds up our faith. Believing the Word of God increases our faith. Walking in faith like the Bible heroes in Hebrews chapter 11 is a powerful way to avoid the enemy's traps.

Weapon Five: Prayer and Fasting

Prayer is a very strong weapon against the enemy. And prayer with fasting is a deadly combination-a powerful combination against our enemy. Many times the hold of the enemy upon our lives can only be broken by prayer and fasting. While you are fasting it may seem as if nothing is happening, but there are powerful things being broken in the spiritual realm. Many times just a simple 24-hour fast is enough to break the hold of the enemy upon our lives. Sometimes more is required-seek God and ask Him how long and what kind of fast He wants you to go on. Fasting on a regular basis will keep evil at a distance and strongholds broken down in your life. It is a way of saying and showing God that you are willing to give up feeding your flesh and you are putting Him first in your life. The enemy of our soul-the devil really hates that because he knows it is a sure way of resisting and defeating him. Don't underestimate the power of praying and fasting. If you are not living a life of fasting, I would encourage you to consider making it a top priority, along with praying, and see what happens!

Weapon Six: The Name of Jesus

There is power in the name of Jesus-when we use that name against the devil he must flee.

- Philippians 2:9–11 says, "Therefore God also has highly exalted Him and given Him the name which is above every name, that at the name of Jesus every knee should bow, of those in heaven, and of those on earth, and of those under the earth, and that every tongue should confess that Jesus Christ is Lord, to the glory of God the Father."

We receive forgiveness of our sins, deliverance from the evil one, healing for our bodies, and the baptism of the Holy Spirit through the name of Jesus. Physical healings were manifested when the disciples used the name of Jesus. There is healing power in the name of Jesus.

- Acts 2:38 says, "Peter replied, "Each of you must turn from your sins and turn to God, and be baptized in the name of Jesus Christ for the forgiveness of your sins. Then you will receive the gift of the Holy Spirit."
- Acts 3:6 says, "But Peter said, "I don't have any money for you. But I'll give you what I have. In the name of Jesus Christ of Nazareth, get up and walk" (NLT)!

God has given us, His children, permission to use the name of Jesus against our enemy. God the father stands behind the name of Jesus and honors that name when we use it against the devil.

Weapon Seven: Our Testimony

Revelation 12:11 says, "And they have defeated him because of the blood of the Lamb and because of their testimony." We overcome or defeat the enemy by our testimony. Each one of us has a powerful testimony of how Jesus has helped us overcome the temptations of the devil and remain strong and steadfast in the Lord and in His Word. The enemy does not like it when we testify about what the Lord has done for us. Our testimony encourages others and helps to build up their faith.

Step Three: Remain in His Love

In John 15:4–13 Jesus talks about abiding (remaining) in Him! In order to bear fruit we must abide (remain) in Him. Without Him we can do nothing. If we do not abide or remain connected to Him we can do nothing, but if we abide or remain in Him we will bear much fruit. If we stay joined or connected to Him and His Word abides in our hearts we can ask any request we desire, and it will be granted to us. The Father is glorified when we bear much fruit. Jesus tells us to abide, stay, and remain in His love in verse 9. When we obey Him, we abide or remain in His love. Jesus told us this so that His joy would remain in us and that joy would be complete and that our joy would overflow to others.

Paul tells us in 1 Corinthians 13:13 that there are three things that will abide, endure, or remain-faith, hope, and charity (love), but the greatest of these is charity (love). In order to be in God's presence all the time, we must walk the love walk at all times. When we walk in divine love, we will be in the presence of the Lord God Almighty more consistently.

Step Four: Walk in Peace with Everyone

Keep your mind stayed upon the Lord all day long! Walking in peace each and every day also keeps us in the presence of our Lord. This is not an easy task, is it? To abide or remain in His presence, we must pursue peace; we must strive to live at peace with everyone!

- Psalm 34:14 says, "Depart from evil and do good; seek peace and pursue it."
- Isaiah 26:3 says, "You will keep him in perfect peace, whose mind is stayed on you, because he trusts in you."
- Jesus tells us in Mark 9:50 to live in peace with one another.
- Jesus was a promoter of peace because He was the prince of peace (Isaiah 9:6). Jesus said in John 14:27, "Peace I leave with you, My peace I give to you; not as the world gives do I give to you. Let not your heart be troubled, neither let it be afraid."
- In him (Jesus) we can have peace. John 16:33 says, "These things I have spoken to you, that in Me you may have peace. In the world you will have tribulation; but be of good cheer, I have overcome the world."
- We have peace with God through our Lord Jesus Christ (Romans 5:1).

- In 2 Corinthians 13:11, the apostle Paul admonishes us to "live in harmony and peace. Then the God of love and peace will be with you." He instructs us to live in peace and harmony with one another and then the love of God and the peace of God will be with us.
- Peace is a fruit of the spirit (Galatians 5:22).
- Paul tells us in Colossians 3:15 that we are all called to live in peace. "And let the peace that comes from Christ rule in your hearts. For as members of one body you are all called to live in peace. And always be thankful."
- Paul tells us again in 1 Thessalonians 5:13 to live peaceably with one another.
- Again we are told to pursue peace in 2 Timothy 2:22: "Flee also youthful lusts; but pursue righteousness, faith, love, peace with those who call on the Lord out of a pure heart."
- Hebrews 12:14: "Pursue peace with all people, and holiness, without which no one will see the Lord."
- 1 Peter 3:11: "Let him turn away from evil and do good; Let him seek peace and pursue it."

Step Five: Stay out of Strife

Stay out of strife! Refuse to get into strife with anyone. We are still worldly minded when we get into envy, strife, and divisions.

- 1 Corinthians 3:3 says, "You are still worldly. For since there is jealousy and quarreling among you, are you not worldly? Are you not acting like mere men" (NIV)?
- Romans 13:13–14, says, "Let us walk properly, as in the day, not in revelry and drunkenness, not in lewdness and lust, not in strife and envy. But put on the Lord Jesus Christ, and make no provision for the flesh, to fulfill its lusts."

Paul tells us to walk properly or behave decently, not in strife and envy along with all the other things mentioned in this Scripture. Then he tells us in verse 14 that we are to put on or clothe ourselves with the Lord Jesus Christ and then we will not fulfill the lusts of our flesh—we will not be thinking about how to gratify the desires of our sinful nature. We will not think of ways to indulge our evil desires. Putting on the Lord Jesus Christ means to follow in His footsteps—to think, to act, and to speak as He did!

The Righteousness of Christ

So ask Jesus, through the Holy Spirit, to help you walk in love and walk in peace every day. Walking in love and abiding in peace and tranquility with others each and every day keeps us abiding in His presence. It is so very important and vital to us that we strive to stay at peace and walk in love with others at all times. When we lose our peace and walk out of love we cannot stay or abide in the presence of our Lord. Remember what Paul tells us in Romans 14:17 that the kingdom of God is righteousness, peace and joy in the Holy Spirit. To stay or abide in His presence every day, every hour, every minute of that day, we have that righteousness that comes through Jesus Christ our Lord. By grace we are saved and made the righteousness of God through Jesus Christ our Lord so we now have right standing with God.

- 2 Corinthians 5:21 says, "God made him who had no sin to be sin for us, so that in him we might become the righteousness of God."
- In Psalm 11:7 David tells us that the Lord loves righteousness, "For the LORD is righteous, He loves righteousness; His countenance beholds the upright."
- Psalm 23:3 tells us that He leads us in paths of righteousness for His name's sake.
- King David tells us in Psalms 111:3, 112:3 and 112:9 that His righteousness endures forever.
- His righteousness is an everlasting righteousness. (Psalm 119:142).
- Proverbs 2:20 tells us to keep to the paths of righteousness or stay on the paths of the righteous.
- Proverbs 11:18–19 tells us that he who sows righteousness will have a sure reward. "As righteousness leads to life" then living in His righteousness has a reward and it leads to life.
- The Lord loves those who pursue righteousness. (Proverbs 15:9).
- Proverbs 21:21 says, "He who follows righteousness and mercy finds life, righteousness and honor."
- We are covered by the robe of His righteousness (Isaiah 61:10).
- Jesus said in Matthew 5:21, "For I say to you, that unless your righteousness exceeds the righteousness of the scribes and Pharisees, you will by no means enter the kingdom of heaven."

- Jesus also tells us in Matthew 6:33 to seek His righteousness, "But seek first the kingdom of God and His righteousness, and all these things shall be added to you."
- Because we have been set free from sin, we have become the slaves of righteousness. We must choose to be slaves to righteousness so that we can become holy. (Romans 6:18–19).
- "God made him who had no sin to be sin for us, so that in him we might become the righteousness of God" (2 Corinthians 5:21 NIV).
- "We have righteousness as our weapon, both to attack and to defend ourselves" (2 Corinthians 6:7 NLT).
- "You must display a new nature because you are a new person, created in God's likeness--righteous, holy, and true" (Ephesians 4:24 NLT).
- Paul tells us in 1 Timothy 6:11 and in 2 Timothy 2:22 to pursue righteousness.
- The crown of righteousness awaits us when Jesus returns! (2 Timothy 4:8).
- 1 John 3:7 says, "Little children, let no one deceive you. He who practices righteousness is righteous, just as He is righteous."

Step Six: Joy

If we want to stay in the presence of the Lord, we must not allow anyone or anything to steal our joy!

- The joy of the Lord is our strength (Nehemiah 8:10).
- King David in Psalm 5:11 says, "But let all who take refuge in you rejoice; let them sing joyful praises forever. Protect them, so all who love your name may be filled with joy" (NLT).
- In God's presence there is fullness of joy (Psalm 16:11).
- "Weeping may go on all night, but joy comes with the morning."(Psalm 30:5).
- "So rejoice in the LORD and be glad, all you who obey him! Shout for joy, all you whose hearts are pure"(Psalm 32:11)!
- "Sing to him a new song; play skillfully, and shout for joy"(Psalm 33:3, NIV).
- God is the source of all joy (Psalm 43:4).
- "Restore to me again the joy of your salvation, and make me willing to obey you" (Psalm 51:12 NLT).
- "Those who sow in tears will reap with songs of joy" (Psalm 126:5 NIV).

- We are to live in joy and peace (Isaiah 55:12).
- He can give us joy instead of mourning (Isaiah 61:3).
- The words of the Lord sustain us and bring us great joy and cause our hearts to rejoice (Jeremiah 15:16).
- "Yet I will rejoice in the LORD, I will joy in the God of my salvation. The LORD God is my strength; He will make my feet like deer's feet, and He will make me walk on my high hills" (Habakkuk 3:18–19).
- Jesus tells us in John 15:11 that the joy of the Lord is supposed to remain or abide in us and that our joy should be full, complete, and overflowing, "These things I have spoken to you, that My joy may remain in you, and that your joy may be full."
- God filled the disciples or believers with joy in Acts 13:52: "And the disciples were filled with joy and with the Holy Spirit."
- Paul prayed for the believers in Rome to be filled with joy and peace: "May the God of hope fill you with all joy and peace as you trust in him, so that you may overflow with hope by the power of the Holy Spirit" (Romans 15:13).
- Joy is a fruit of the spirit (Galatians 5:22).
- In Colossians 1:11 Paul prayed for the believers to be filled with joy, "We also pray that you will be strengthened with his glorious power so that you will have all the patience and endurance you need. May you be filled with joy."
- James tells us in James 1:2 that whenever trouble comes to let it be an opportunity for joy, "Consider it pure joy, my brothers, whenever you face trials of many kinds."
- Peter 1:8 tells us to be filled with an inexpressible and glorious joy, "Though you have not seen him, you love him; and even though you do not see him now, you believe in him and are filled with an inexpressible and glorious joy."

To remain, abide or stay in His presence, we must do that which is right and good, walk in peace with all men at all times, and let the joy of the Lord be our strength. Don't let the devil steal your joy. It will be obvious to others that we abide in the presence of our Lord when we walk in love, walk in peace, and have the joy of the Lord each and every day. The Bible tells us to rejoice in the Lord always and again I say rejoice (Philippians 4:4). Always be full of joy in the Lord! In order for us to remain or abide in the presence of God, we must not complain, find fault or argue with others. There can be no strife in our lives.

- Philippians 2:14 says, "In everything you do, stay away from complaining and arguing" (NLT).

Step Seven: Forgiveness

To abide or stay in the presence of God, we cannot allow any unforgiveness to creep into our lives. Forgiveness is a choice-we choose to forgive others and if we refuse to forgive others our heavenly Father will not forgive us. Consider what each of the following Scriptures tell us about forgiveness.

- Matthew 6:12–15: "and forgive us our sins, just as we have forgiven those who have sinned against us. And don't let us yield to temptation, but deliver us from the evil one. If you forgive those who sin against you, your heavenly Father will forgive you. But if you refuse to forgive others, your Father will not forgive your sins" (NLT).
- If we forgive others, God will forgive us. Luke 6:37 says, "Stop judging others and you will not be judged. Stop criticizing others, or it will all come back on you. If you forgive others, you will be forgiven" (NLT).
- Ephesians 4:30–5:2 says, "And do not bring sorrow to God's Holy Spirit by the way you live. Remember, he is the one who has identified you as his own, guaranteeing that you will be saved on the day of redemption. Get rid of all bitterness, rage, anger, harsh words, and slander, as well as all types of malicious behavior. Instead, be kind to each other, tenderhearted, forgiving one another, just as God through Christ has forgiven you. Follow God's example in everything you do, because you are his dear children. Live a life filled with love for others, following the example of Christ, who loved you and gave himself as a sacrifice to take away your sins" (NLT).
- Colossians 3:12–15 says, "Since God chose you to be the holy people whom he loves, you must clothe yourselves with tenderhearted mercy, kindness, humility, gentleness, and patience. You must make allowance for each other's faults and forgive the person who offends you. Remember, the Lord forgave you, so you must forgive others. And the most important piece of clothing you must wear is love. Love is what binds us all together in perfect harmony. And let the peace that comes from Christ rule in your hearts. For as members of one body you are all called to live in peace. And always be thankful" (NLT).

Be quick to forgive! Staying or abiding in the presence of God is by no means easy. But, I believe if we take one day at a time and make that our goal for that day we can remain in His presence! Abiding in the presence of God is very rewarding and satisfying to our spirits.

When we abide in the presence of the Lord all day long, our spirit is calm, at rest, peaceful and content. His joy gives us strength—His strength! When we are in the presence of the Lord, we are carefree! We are free from the cares of this world and free from worry, and anxiety. When we are in His presence, we are stress free—no more stress in our lives. Life is good; life is great; life is enjoyable. We begin to enjoy our lives and enjoy being alive. We look forward to each new day so that we can abide with Him, talk to Him, work for Him, and sup with Him.

Once we get into His presence, we just need to abide and stay there for awhile. Too often we are in a big hurry to leave His presence. It is so glorious, so heavenly that we will want to stay there forever—to never leave the banqueting table. One of our spiritual goals should be to eat and sup with Him all the days of our lives. Abiding or staying in His presence once we get there allows us to do just that! Will you make it a spiritual goal to get into His presence and then abide there for awhile?

Conclusion

Prayer

Our dear Heavenly Father, help us to praise until we worship, worship until we enter into your presence and then stand in your presence! Thank you Jesus for your presence in our daily lives as we take one day at a time. You are in control of everything and we submit and surrender our hearts, souls, and bodies to you this day and every day. May everything we say and do this day bring glory and honor unto you! You are the King of Kings and Lord of Lords. You are master controller of our lives, and we love you and want to serve you all the days of our lives. Help us to do everything this day as unto the Lord, and for the Lord. We want to abide in your presence all the days of our lives, but we need the help of the Holy Spirit to do that. Help us to abide in your presence this day. Thank you so much for your unconditional love, your peace that passes all understanding and the joy of the Lord which gives us strength. We believe that miracles happen when we get into your presence to abide and stay there. We need your glory to fall on us today! In Jesus name we pray, amen.

Chapter Four

Review Questions

1. Do you think it is possible to abide or stay in the presence of the Lord when life is difficult or hard? If so how?

2. What authority do you have over your enemy the devil as a believer?

3. Name the seven weapons of our warfare that we can use against Satan.
    1.)
    2.)
    3.)
    4.)
    5.)
    6.)
    7.)

4. Give the definition of what it means to abide.

5. What does the word *stay* mean as it regards to the presence of the Lord?

6. The apostle Paul tells us in _____ that there are three things that abide, endure, or remain. What are they?
    1.)
    2.)
    3.)

7. Quote and memorize Isaiah 26:3.

8. Paul tells us in Romans 14:17 that the kingdom of God is _____, _____, and _____ in the Holy Spirit.

9. Give at least three Scripture references and write them out that speak of our righteousness that we now have in Christ Jesus.
    1.)
    2.)
    3.)

10. To abide or remain in His presence we must pursue _____; we must strive to walk in _____ with everyone.

11. If we want to stay in the presence of the Lord we must not allow anyone or anything to steal our _____.

12. Quote at least three Scriptures that speak about *JOY*. Memorize one of them!
    1.)
    2.)
    3.)

13. _____ says "in everything you do, stay away from complaining and arguing."

14. In order to stay or abide in the presence of an Almighty God, we cannot allow any _____ to creep into our hearts.

15. We need to be _____ to forgive.

16. Abiding in the presence of the Lord is by no means easy. What are some of the benefits to our spirits when we take one day at a time and stay in the presence of the Lord all day long?

    1.)

    2.)

    3.)

17. Write out a prayer in your own words asking God to help you abide in His presence today.

Divine Revelation in the Presence of The Lord God Almighty

Review of Chapter Four

We began chapter four explaining how we can stay or abide in the presence of an Almighty God at all times. I reminded you not to forget the authority you have as a believer over your enemy. We also discussed the top seven weapons of our warfare against Satan. I discussed with you what it means to abide or stay in the presence of the Lord. Abiding in His presence can be very rewarding and satisfying to our spirits. I believe with the Lord's help and divine revelation we can get to that place where we abide in the presence of an Almighty God more and more!

We will begin this chapter with a definition of divine revelation from the dictionary and from the Bible. Then we will discuss how we go about getting this divine revelation from God.

Definition of Divine Revelation

Webster's Definition of revelation:
- A revealing or disclosing.
- Something disclosed; disclosure; especially, a striking disclosure, as of something not previously known or realized.

In Christian theology:
- God's disclosure or manifestation to His creatures of Himself and His will.
- Something, as the Bible, containing such disclosure or manifestation.
- The last book of the New Testament, ascribed to John (The Revelation of Saint John the Divine)

Webster's definition of divine:

- Of or like God or a god;
- Given or inspired by God; holy; sacred;
- Devoted to God; religious;
- Having to do with theology;
- Supremely great, good, etc;
- Very pleasing, attractive;
- Divinity: a clergyman, a theologian: a person who is a student of or an authority on theology or a theology.
- Theology: the study of God, and the relations between God and the universe; study of religious doctrines and matters of divinity.

Biblical Definition:

- Revelation: from God, by dream or vision.
- Divine: given or inspired by God; holy; sacred.

What does the Bible say about Divine Revelation?

- Proverbs 16:10 says, "The king speaks with divine wisdom; he must never judge unfairly" (NLT).
- Hebrews 9:1 says, "Then verily the first covenant had also ordinances of divine service, and a worldly sanctuary" (KJV). The NLT says, "Now in that first covenant between God and Israel, there were regulations for worship and a sacred tent here on earth (NIV "an earthly sanctuary").
- 2 Peter 1:3–8 says, "His divine power has given us everything we need for life and godliness through our knowledge of him who called us by his own glory and goodness. Through these he has given us his very great and precious promises, so that through them you may participate in the divine nature and escape the corruption in the world caused by evil desires. For this very reason, make every effort to add to your faith goodness; and to goodness, knowledge; and to knowledge, self-control; and to self-control, perseverance; and to perseverance, godliness; and to godliness, brotherly kindness; and to brotherly kindness, love. For if you possess these qualities in increasing measure, they will keep you from being ineffective and unproductive in your knowledge of our Lord Jesus Christ" (NIV).

- Proverbs 29:18 says, "When people do not accept divine guidance, they run wild. But whoever obeys the law is happy" (NLT).
- Jeremiah 5:13 says, "God's prophets are windbags full of words with no divine authority. Their predictions of disaster will fall on themselves" (NLT)!
- Daniel 3:25 says, "Look! Nebuchadnezzar shouted. I see four men, unbound, walking around in the fire. They aren't even hurt by the flames! And the fourth looks like a divine being" (NLT)!
- Daniel 5:12 says, "This man Daniel, whom the king named Belteshazzar, has a sharp mind and is filled with divine knowledge and understanding. He can interpret dreams, explain riddles, and solve difficult problems. Call for Daniel, and he will tell you what the writing means" (NLT).
- Romans 1:20 says, "From the time the world was created, people have seen the earth and sky and all that God made. They can clearly see his invisible qualities--his eternal power and divine nature. So they have no excuse whatsoever for not knowing God" (NLT).
- 2 Peter 1:2–3 says, "As we know Jesus better, his divine power gives us everything we need for living a godly life. He has called us to receive his own glory and goodness! And by that same mighty power, he has given us all of his rich and wonderful promises. He has promised that you will escape the decadence all around you caused by evil desires and that you will share in his divine nature" (NLT).

How Do We Receive Divine Revelation from the Lord?

Pray for Divine Revelation

This is God's will for us, to understand and comprehend his divine Word.

- Psalm 119:18 says, "Open my eyes, that I may see wondrous things from your law." Pray this Scripture before you start reading the Bible and ask God for divine revelation and that God would give you a rhema Word!
- Pray the prayer Paul prayed in Ephesians 1:17–23: "that the God of our Lord Jesus Christ, the Father of glory, may give to you the spirit of wisdom and revelation in the knowledge of Him, the eyes of your understanding being enlightened; that you may know what is the hope of His calling, what are the riches of the glory of His inheritance in the saints, and what is the exceeding

greatness of His power toward us who believe, according to the working of His mighty power which He worked in Christ when He raised Him from the dead and seated Him at His right hand in the heavenly places, far above all principality and power and might and dominion, and every name that is named, not only in this age but also in that which is to come. And He put all things under His feet, and gave Him to be head over all things to the church, which is His body, the fullness of Him who fills all in all."

- Colossians 1:9 says, "For this reason we also, since the day we heard it, do not cease to pray for you, and to ask that you may be filled with the knowledge of His will in all wisdom and spiritual understanding;"

The Holy Spirit speaks to our spirit about what the Word is saying to us. Allow the Holy Spirit to speak to your spirit about what the Word is saying to you when you read it. This is called a *rhema* Word!

Seek After the Baptism of the Holy Spirit

When you become a believer by asking Jesus to come into you heart, and make Him Lord of your life, you are at that time filled with the Holy Spirit. The Holy Spirit dwells inside of you, but in order to have a greater understanding concerning the Word of God, we need to be baptized in the Holy Spirit with the evidence of speaking in tongues.

Jesus was filled with the Holy Spirit. Luke 4:1 says, "Then Jesus, being filled with the Holy Spirit, returned from the Jordan and was led by the Spirit into the wilderness." If Jesus was filled with the Holy Spirit then, in the days we are living in, we need all the help we can get from God to do and say the things that Jesus did and said.

- Acts 2:1–4 says, "When the Day of Pentecost had fully come, they were all with one accord in one place. And suddenly there came a sound from heaven, as of a rushing mighty wind, and it filled the whole house where they were sitting. Then there appeared to them divided tongues, as of fire, and one sat upon each of them. And they were all filled with the Holy Spirit and began to speak with other tongues, as the Spirit gave them utterance."

- Acts 4:31 says, "And when they had prayed, the place where they were assembled together was shaken; and they were all filled with the Holy Spirit, and they spoke the word of God with boldness."

The Holy Spirit imparts divine revelation into our spirits when we ask Him to. He is a perfect gentleman and will not do anything unless we ask Him to do it for us. Our part is to want what God wants for us—to do the will of the Father. It is God's will for us according to His Word that we be filled with the Holy Spirit with the evidence of speaking with tongues.

Recently, in our Thursday morning ladies' Bible study, when we had invited the Holy Spirit to honor us with His presence, each and every person in that Bible study received or got more and more divine revelation (a better understanding of His Word). It is so exciting and important that we seek after and receive God's divine revelation so that we can disciple others and help them to better understand God's Word. When we are in the presence of our Lord God Almighty as we study God's Word together, divine revelation is imparted to us from our Heavenly Father. It is my deepest desire that every time I open the Word of God that God reveals Himself to me more and more and gives me a better and greater understanding of who He is and what He expects of me.

Guard Your Minds and Hearts

I have prayed and asked God Almighty to impart more divine revelation into my mind. Our minds are the most complex computer in the world. It is essential that we guard our minds and hearts with all diligence. What does the Bible say about our minds? If you have not read Joyce Meyer's best-selling book *Battlefield of the Mind* you really should do so, and read it more than once, because most of the battles we have with our enemy, Satan, are in the mind.

Here are some Bible verses on the mind and heart:

- Genesis 37:11 says, "But while his brothers were jealous of Joseph, his father gave it some thought and wondered what it all meant" (NLT).
- 1 Samuel 2:35 says, "Then I will rise up for myself a faithful priest who shall do according to what is in my heart and in my mind. I will build him a sure house, and he shall walk before my anointed forever."

- 1 Chronicles 28:9 says, "As for you, my son Solomon, know the God of your father, and serve Him with a loyal heart and with a willing mind; for the LORD searches all hearts and understands all the intent of the thoughts. If you seek Him, He will be found by you; but if you forsake Him, He will cast you off forever."

In 1 Chronicles, above, the Bible speaks of a loyal heart and a willing mind. Notice that the writer of this book inspired by the Holy Spirit said a loyal heart first and then a willing mind will follow. The heart or spirit should be in charge directing the mind, not the other way around. Just as we serve out of a heart of love a Triune God-Father, Son, and Holy Ghost, so likewise, we consist of three parts-body, soul, and spirit. The body is the physical part of us. The soul consists of the mind, the will, and the emotions. And the spirit or heart is where the Holy Spirit takes up residence or abides (stays).

Remember that your body houses the Holy Spirit of God, so treat it as a temple not a garbage dump. Let's take a look at some Scriptures to get a better understanding about what I am talking about.

- 1 Corinthians 6:19–20 says, "What? Know ye not that your body is the temple of the Holy Ghost which is in you, which ye have of God, and ye are not your own? For ye are bought with a price: therefore glorify God in your body, and in your spirit, which are God's" (KJV).
- Psalm 79:1 says, "O God, pagan nations have conquered your land, your special possession. They have defiled your holy Temple and made Jerusalem a heap of ruins" (KJV).

Just like the pagan nations conquered the land of Israel and defiled the temple of the Lord, so likewise, we have allowed pagan religions to come into the United States of America and they have brought with them their gods—Buddha, Mohammad, New Age, witchcraft, Satan worshipers, the Masons, and all kinds of false religions and cults—thus causing our temples (our churches) to be defiled with their pagan gods, false teachings, and non-Biblical beliefs and influences. Our children are introduced to these gods at a very early age through public media, the public schools, and by establishing friendships with children who are taught these false religions. We, as born again believers, need to be aware of what our children and grandchildren are seeing, hearing, and doing, and the friendships they are developing in the public schools.

Things have changed so rapidly in the last 40 to 50 years because Satan knows his time is running out, and that Jesus Christ our Lord and Savior is coming back soon. Satan has increased his influence in our families' lives more than ever before! Stand strong against these evil things in the name of Jesus and by the power of the blood of the Lamb. Apply the blood of Jesus to the mind, will, and emotions of your children and grandchildren. They need to be protected by the blood of Jesus and the name of Jesus! Let Satan know that the blood of Jesus is against him! We overcome evil with good, not more evil. That is why there is so much evil in the world today, because we (even the so called believers) are overcoming evil with evil instead of overcoming evil with good, as the Bible commands us to do! Romans 12:21 says, "Be not overcome of evil, but overcome evil with good."

What Kind of Mind Do We Need to Have to Receive Divine Revelation from God?

1. A Made Up Mind

- Nehemiah 4:6 says, "So we built the wall, and the entire wall was joined together up to half its height, for the people had a mind to work."

The people here had a made up mind-a mind to work. They decided to build the wall and nothing or no one was going to stop them. When God tells you to do something, have a made up mind that you are going to do what God tells you to do exactly the way He tells you to do it, and don't let anything or anybody get in your way to stop you from being obedient to God.

2. A Peaceful, Quiet Mind

- Isaiah 26:3 says, "You will keep him in perfect peace, Whose mind is stayed on You, Because he trusts in You. Trust in the LORD forever, For in YAH, the LORD, is everlasting strength."
- Philippians 4: 5–8 says, "Be anxious for nothing, but in everything by prayer and supplication, with thanksgiving, let your requests be made known to God; and the peace of God, which surpasses all understanding, will guard

your hearts and minds through Christ Jesus. Finally, brethren, whatever things are true, whatever things are noble, whatever things are just, whatever things are pure, whatever things are lovely, whatever things are of good report, if there is any virtue and if there is anything praiseworthy; meditate on these things." The Word of God is very specific on what we are to think on here!

- 1 Peter 5:7 says, "Give all your worries and cares to God, for he cares about what happens to you" (NLT). We should live carefree lives-casting or throwing all of our worries, all of our anxieties, all of our concerns on the Lord.

- Luke 12:29 says, "And don't worry about food--what to eat and drink. Don't worry whether God will provide it for you."

3. *Minds that Meditate on the Word of God and the Good Things God Has Done for Us*

- Matthew 22:37 says, "Jesus said to him, 'you shall love the LORD your God with all your heart, with all your soul, and with all your mind.'"

- Mark 12:30 says, "And you shall love the LORD your God with all your heart, with all your soul, with all your mind, and with all your strength. This is the first commandment."

- Luke 10:27 says, "So he answered and said, 'You shall love the LORD your God with all your heart, with all your soul, with all your strength, and with all your mind, and your neighbor as yourself.'"

4. *One Mind in One Accord with the Body of Christ*

- 1 Chronicles 12:38 says, "All these were fighting men who volunteered to serve in the ranks. They came to Hebron fully determined to make David king over all Israel. All the rest of the Israelites were also of one mind to make David king" (NIV).

- Romans 15:5–6 says, "Now may the God of patience and comfort grant you to be like-minded toward one another, according to Christ Jesus that you may with one mind and one mouth glorify the God and Father of our Lord Jesus Christ."

- 1 Corinthians 1:10 says, "Now, dear brothers and sisters, I appeal to you by the authority of the Lord Jesus Christ to stop arguing among yourselves. Let there be real harmony so there won't be divisions in the church. I plead with you to be of one mind, united in thought and purpose" (NLT).
- 2 Corinthians 13:11 says, "Finally, brethren, farewell. Become complete. Be of good comfort, be of one mind, live in peace; and the God of love and peace will be with you."
- Philippians 1:27 says, "Only let your conduct be worthy of the gospel of Christ, so that whether I come and see you or am absent, I may hear of your affairs, that you stand fast in one spirit, with one mind striving together for the faith of the gospel."

5. A Right Mind

- Mark 5:15 says, "Then they came to Jesus, and saw the one who had been demon-possessed and had the legion, sitting and clothed and in his right mind. And they were afraid."
- Luke 8:35 says, "Then they went out to see what was done; and came to Jesus, and found the man, out of whom the devils were departed, sitting at the feet of Jesus, clothed, and in his right mind: and they were afraid" (KJV).
- 2 Corinthians. 5:13 says, "If it seems that we are crazy, it is to bring glory to God. And if we are in our right minds, it is for your benefit" (NLT).
- 2 Timothy 1:7 says, "For God has not given us a spirit of fear, but of power and of love and of a sound mind."

6. A Ready mind

- 2 Corinthians 8:19 says, "And not that only, but who was also chosen of the churches to travel with us with this grace, which is administered by us to the glory of the same Lord, and declaration of your ready mind" (KJV).
- 1 Peter 5:2 says, "Feed the flock of God which is among you, taking the oversight thereof, not by constraint, but willingly; not for filthy lucre, but of a ready mind" (KJV).

Mary L. Hock

What Kind of Heart Do We Need to Have to Receive Divine Revelation from God?

The heart is the place where the Spirit of God resides or abides. The intents or conditions of the heart are an evil heart and a good heart.

1. An Evil Heart

An evil heart is a hard heart that the Word cannot penetrate: A hard-hearted person; controlled by demonic influences; not obedient to the Word of God or the spirit of God; disobedient. Ungrateful, unforgiving, bitter, resentful, does not trust anyone, even God Almighty, lies, steals, murders, cheats. Deceives others, sneaky, sly, proud, jealous, envious, selfish, cold, incapable of loving with an agape kind of love, their love is conditional, up to no good, malicious, hateful, violent, rude, unreasonable, confused, tormented, fearful, lustful, seducing, greedy, taker and not a giver, stingy, idol worshiper, backbiting, gossiping, unwholesome tongue-not able to control their tongues, men pleasers not God pleasers, totally messed up!

2. A Good Heart

A good heart is pleasant, kind, loving-unconditional love, loves the unlovable, compassionate, merciful, humble, loves God and puts Him first always, passionate, forgiving, cheerful giver, pure, righteous-always wants to do the right thing no matter what it costs, sensitive, grateful or thankful, honorable, respectful, useful, helpful, servants, a blessing to others, gives praise to God and others, considerate, caring, sharing, and generous.

What Kind of Fruit Do These Two Hearts Produce?

The Fruit of an Evil Heart

An evil heart is not good, it is rotten, spoiled, sour, harmful, lazy, distasteful, nauseating, sinful, non-productive, negative, and dead!

- Matthew 7:18–20 says, "A good tree can't produce bad fruit, and a bad tree can't produce good fruit. So every tree that does not produce good fruit is chopped down and thrown into the fire. Yes, the way to identify a tree or a person is by the kind of fruit that is produced" (NLT).

- Matthew 3:10 says, "And even now the ax is laid to the root of the trees. Therefore every tree which does not bear good fruit is cut down and thrown into the fire."

The Fruit of a Good Heart

A good heart tastes good, it is active, energetic, pleasant, desirable, tasty, delicious, productive, positive, and living; not dead!

- Galatians 5:22–23 says, "But when the Holy Spirit controls our lives, he will produce this kind of fruit in us: love, joy, peace, patience, kindness, goodness, faithfulness, gentleness, and self-control" (NLT).
- Ephesians 5:9 says "(for the fruit of the Spirit is in all goodness, righteousness, and truth)."
- John 15:8 says, "By this My Father is glorified, that you bear much fruit; so you will be My disciples." Verse 16 says, "You did not choose Me, but I chose you and appointed you that you should go and bear fruit, and that your fruit should remain, that whatever you ask the Father in My name He may give you."

It would be beneficial for you to read all of John 15:1–27! Jesus has much to say about the condition of our hearts in this chapter in the Bible.

Scripture References about the Two Different Kinds of Hearts

1. The Bad Heart or Evil Heart

- Genesis 6:5–6 says, "Then the LORD saw that the wickedness of man was great in the earth, and that every intent of the thoughts of his heart was only evil continually. And the LORD was sorry that He had made man on the earth, and He was grieved in His heart."
- Exodus 7:14 says, "So the LORD said to Moses: "Pharaoh's heart is hard; he refuses to let the people go."
- Exodus 7:22–23 says, "Then the magicians of Egypt did so with their enchantments; and Pharaoh's heart grew hard, and he did not heed them, as

the LORD had said. And Pharaoh turned and went into his house. Neither was his heart moved by this."

- Exodus 8:19 says, "Then the magicians said to Pharaoh, 'This is the finger of God.' But Pharaoh's heart grew hard, and he did not heed them, just as the LORD had said."
- Exodus 9:7 says, "Then Pharaoh sent, and indeed, not even one of the livestock of the Israelites was dead. But the heart of Pharaoh became hard, and he did not let the people go."
- Exodus 9:12 says, "But the LORD hardened the heart of Pharaoh; and he did not heed them, just as the LORD had spoken to Moses."

There are several references in the Bible in the book of Exodus where the Lord hardened the heart of the Pharaoh and he would not be obedient to the Word of the Lord. This is what happens to us also, if we are not obedient to the Word of God or listen to the voice of God and are disobedient. Then our hearts will become hard and callous so that we can't receive anything from the Lord.

2. *The Good Heart is a Pure Heart*

- Psalm 24:3–4 says, "Who may ascend into the hill of the LORD? Or who may stand in His holy place? He who has clean hands and a pure heart, who has not lifted up his soul to an idol, nor sworn deceitfully."
- 1 Timothy 1:5 says, "The purpose of my instruction is that all the Christians there would be filled with love that comes from a pure heart, a clear conscience, and sincere faith" (NLT).
- 2 Timothy 2:22 says, "Run from anything that stimulates youthful lust. Follow anything that makes you want to do right. Pursue faith and love and peace, and enjoy the companionship of those who call on the Lord with pure hearts" (NLT).
- 1 Peter 1:22 says, "Since you have purified your souls in obeying the truth through the Spirit in sincere love of the brethren, love one another fervently with a pure heart."

On the other hand, the person who has a good heart, an innocent or pure heart, will follow hard after the things of God. These people who pursue God with a passion, with a pure heart, will be obedient to the Word of God and the spirit of

God. Thus, God will bless that individual for serving Him out of a heart that is good, and pure. Pray and ask God Almighty to give you a pure heart, a heart that is soft and pliable so that the Word of God can penetrate it and dominate your life! Listen to and be obedient to that still small voice which is the Holy Spirit talking to you and be obedient immediately to the Word of God and to the Spirit of God. Be submissive and yield your spirit to God's spirit. Get the mind of Christ on everything you do. Walk in obedience and have a blessed life. Listen to your heart, and not to your head or your feelings because they will both get you into trouble and take you places you do not need or really want to go.

- Proverbs 3:3–8 says, "Never let loyalty and kindness get away from you! Wear them like a necklace; write them deep within your heart. Then you will find favor with both God and people, and you will gain a good reputation. Trust in the LORD with all your heart; do not depend on your own understanding. Seek his will in all you do, and he will direct your paths. Don't be impressed with your own wisdom. Instead, fear the LORD and turn your back on evil. Then you will gain renewed health and vitality" (NLT).

- Deuteronomy 11:13–17 says, "If you carefully obey all the commands I am giving you today, and if you love the LORD your God with all your heart and soul, and if you worship him, then He will send the rains in their proper seasons so you can harvest crops of grain, grapes for wine, and olives for oil. He will give you lush pastureland for your cattle to graze in, and you yourselves will have plenty to eat. "But do not let your heart turn away from the LORD to worship other gods. If you do, the Lord's anger will burn against you" (NLT).

- Mark 12: 30–31 says, "and you shall love the LORD your God with all your heart, with all your soul, with all your mind (your entire), and with all your strength.' This is the first commandment. "And the second, like it, is this: 'You shall love your neighbor as yourself.' There is no other commandment greater than these."

- Jesus said in Luke 6:45 "A good man out of the good treasure of his heart brings forth good; and an evil man out of the evil treasure of his heart brings forth evil. For out of the abundance of the heart his mouth speaks."

- Again Jesus said in Luke 8:15 "But the seed on good soil stands for those with a noble and good heart, who hear the word, retain it, and by persevering produce a crop" (NIV).

- John 14:27 says, "Peace I leave with you, my peace I give to you; not as the world gives do I give to you. Let not your heart be troubled, neither let it be afraid."
- Acts 2:46 says, "Every day they continued to meet together in the temple courts. They broke bread in their homes and ate together with glad and sincere hearts" (NIV).
- Acts 4:32 says, "All the believers were one in heart and mind. No one claimed that any of his possessions was his own, but they shared everything they had" (NIV).
- Romans 10:6–10 says, "But the righteousness of faith speaks in this way, Do not say in your heart, Who will ascend into heaven? (that is, to bring Christ down from above) or, who will descend into the abyss? (that is, to bring Christ up from the dead). But what does it say? The word is near you, in your mouth and in your heart (that is, the word of faith which we preach): that if you confess with your mouth the Lord Jesus and believe in your heart that God has raised Him from the dead, you will be saved. For with the heart one believes unto righteousness, and with the mouth confession is made unto salvation."

After considering the conditions of our hearts and minds, we need to guard our hearts and our minds too-why? Because in the Bible Jesus said in Matthew12:34–37 "You brood of snakes! How could evil men like you speak what is good and right? For whatever is in your heart determines what you say. A good person produces good words from a good heart, and an evil person produces evil words from an evil heart. And I tell you this that you must give an account on judgment day of every idle word you speak. The words you say now reflect your fate then; either you will be justified by them or you will be condemned" (NLT).

So what are these verses of Scripture saying to us? Whatever is in your heart determines what you will say or speak. The KJV of the Bible says out of the abundance of the heart the mouth speaks. The mouth speaks or says what is put into the heart or your spirit. So we can also see from these verses from the Bible that a good person plus a good heart equals good words. But, on the other hand, an evil person plus an evil heart equals evil words. Do you want or desire to speak evil words to and over people or good words?

Then Jesus tells us that on judgment day we will give an account to God Almighty for every idle word that we speak. And those words will determine your fate or destiny, where you will spend eternity for either you will be justified by them or you will be condemned.

Conclusion

In order to receive divine revelation from God, we must guard our hearts and minds and put our trust and confidence in God alone.

- Micah 7:5 says, "Do not trust in a friend; Do not put your confidence in a companion; Guard the doors of your mouth from her who lies in your bosom." The NLT says, "Don't trust anyone--not your best friend or even your wife!"
- Proverbs 4:23 says, "Above all else, guard your heart, for it affects everything you do" (NLT).
- Psalm 118: 8–9 says, "It is better to trust in the LORD than to put confidence in man. It is better to trust in the LORD than to put confidence in princes."

The Word of God also teaches that His peace can guard our hearts. Philippians 4:6–7 says, "Don't worry about anything; instead, pray about everything. Tell God what you need, and thank him for all he has done. If you do this, you will experience God's peace, which is far more wonderful than the human mind can understand. His peace will guard your hearts and minds as you live in Christ Jesus" (NLT).

Prayer

Lord, we desire to receive divine revelation from You. Help us Lord to guard our hearts and minds. We cast (pitch or throw) all our worries, all our anxieties, all our concerns (list them) upon You for You care for us. You are our burden bearer, our strong tower, and our refuge in the time of need. Because we refuse to worry about anything, but pray about everything, then that peace that passes all understanding will guard our hearts and minds in Christ Jesus. Lord, You are the only one we can trust completely! So we put all of our faith and trust in You and Your Word. You alone are worthy of our praise and worship. Without you we can do nothing. With You we can do all things. In Jesus name we pray. Amen.

Chapter Five

Review Questions

1. Give Webster's definition of divine revelation.

2. Now give the biblical definition of divine revelation: Give at least three Scripture verses to support this.
    1.)
    2.)
    3.)

3. How do we go about getting this divine revelation?

4. As far as divine revelation is concerned, does the baptism of the Holy Spirit aid to rightly divide the Word of truth? If so, how?

5. According to Joyce Meyer the battlefield is in the _____.

6. First Chronicles 28:9, NKJV tells us to serve the God of our fathers with a _____ and a _____.

7. What kind of mind does Nehemiah 4:6 talk about?

8. The Bible teaches us to have a _____ not a confused or worried mind. Why and how do we accomplish this? Give Scripture verses to support your answer.

9. All of our mind should _____ on the Word of God and the good things He has done for us.

10. The Bible promotes that the body of Christ should have unity or be of _____ and walk in harmony with one another. Give two scriptures that teach this. Memorize one of them.
    1.)
    2.)

11. A _____ mind is a sound mind. Give two scripture references that support this.
    1.)
    2.)

12. 2 Corinthians 8:19 and 1 Peter 5:2 both address that we should have a _____ mind.

13. What are the two conditions of the heart? Give an explanation of each one.
    1.)
    2.)

14. What kind of fruit do these two hearts produce? Give a couple of Scriptures to support your answer.
    1.)
    2.)

15. Is it desirable for us to have a hard heart? If not, why not?

16. It is better for us to have an innocent heart or a _____ heart. Why?

17. Why do we need to guard our hearts and our minds?

18. The Word of God teaches us that His _____ can guard our hearts. Write out and memorize the Scripture verses that tell us this.

CHAPTER SIX

Standing in the Presence of the Lord God Almighty

Review of Chapter Five

I started this chapter by giving the definition of divine revelation and showing you what the Bible has to say about it. Then we discussed how we go about obtaining divine revelation. I explained to you the importance of the different heart and mind conditions and what kind of fruit they produce. I concluded this chapter with a prayer asking God Almighty to give us divine revelation.

Introduction to Chapter Six

The Bible teaches us that after we have done everything we know how to do then it is time to just stand your ground and wait. Waiting on the Lord is not easy! We need to learn how to stand in the presence of the Lord God Almighty-to wait on the Lord! In this chapter, I will share with you some of my personal experiences in the last 50 plus years where I was asked by the Lord God Almighty to stand my ground or wait! We will be taking a look at the armor of God found in Ephesians 6:10–20. Put on the whole armor of God every day of your life and be protected from the fiery darts of the wicked one, don't get beat up and wounded all the time-protect yourself with the Word of God. I will also share the plan of salvation with you to give you an opportunity to say a sinner's prayer and become a believer.

We need to put on the whole armor of God daily. Ephesians 6:10–13, says: "Finally, be strong in the Lord and in his mighty power. Put on the full armor of God so that you can take your stand against the devil's schemes. For our struggle is not against flesh and blood, but against the rulers, against the authorities, against the powers of this dark world and against the spiritual forces of evil in the heavenly realms. Therefore put on the full armor of God, so that when the day of evil comes, you may be able to stand your ground, and after you have done everything, to stand" (NIV).

Our Armor

So what are the different parts of this armor that we are to put on daily to protect us from the tricks and schemes of the enemy, Satan?

1. Our Armor: Truth

Ephesians 6:14 says: "Stand firm therefore, having girded your loins with truth" (NASB).

Girded or *gird* means: fastened; buckled; to enclose, surround, to encircle with a belt or band, to fasten with a belt or band; to encircle; to equip; furnish; clothe; to prepare (oneself) for action.

Loins means: the part of the body between the ribs and the hip bones. It is the place where the girdle was worn and the sword was fastened to. The hips and the lower abdomen regarded as a part of the body to be clothed or as the region of strength and procreative power.

- Exodus 22:11 says: "And thus shall ye eat it; with your loins girded, your shoes on your feet, and your staff in your hand; and ye shall eat it in haste: it is the LORD'S Passover" (KJV).
- Jeremiah 13:1 says: "Thus saith the LORD unto me, Go and get thee a linen girdle, and put it upon thy loins, and put it not in water" (KJV).
- Matthew 3:4 says: "And the same John had his raiment of camel's hair, and a leathern girdle about his loins; and his meat was locusts and wild honey" (KJV).

To have the loins girded with truth signified strength in attachment to truth:
- Ephesians 6:14 says: "Stand therefore, having your loins girt about with truth, and having on the breastplate of righteousness" (KJV).
- Isaiah 11:5 says: "And righteousness shall be the girdle of his loins, and faithfulness the girdle of his reins" (KJV).

Truth means: trustworthiness; sincerity; genuineness; honesty; reality; actual existence; that which is true, statement, etc, which accords or agrees with fact or reality; an established or verified fact, principle, etc.; That which is reliable and can be trusted like God's Word which is the absolute truth!

- John 1:14 says, "And the Word was made flesh, and dwelt among us, (and we beheld his glory, the glory as of the only begotten of the Father,) full of grace and truth" (KJV).
- John 4:24 says, "God is a Spirit: and they that worship him must worship him in spirit and in truth" (KJV).
- John 8:32 says, "And you shall know the truth, and the truth shall make you free."
- Ephesians 6:14 says, "Stand your ground, putting on the sturdy belt of truth and the body armor of God's righteousness" (NLT).
- 2 Timothy 2:15 says, "Be diligent to present yourself approved to God, a worker who does not need to be ashamed, rightly dividing the word of truth."
- 1 Peter 1:22 says, "Now that you have purified yourselves by obeying the truth so that you have sincere love for your brothers, love one another deeply, from the heart" (NIV).
- 1 John 1:8 says, "If we say that we have no sin, we deceive ourselves, and the truth is not in us" (KJV).
- 1 John 2:4 says, "He that saith, I know him, and keepeth not his commandments, is a liar, and the truth is not in him" (KJV).
- 1 John 5:6 says: "This is He who came by water and blood; Jesus Christ; not only by water, but by water and blood. And it is the Spirit who bears witness, because the Spirit is truth."
- 2 John 1:3 says, "May grace, mercy, and peace, which come from God our Father and from Jesus Christ his Son, be with us who live in truth and love" (NLT).

2. Our Armor: The Breastplate of Righteousness

Ephesians 6:14 says, "Having put on the breastplate of righteousness" (NASB).

Webster's definition of *righteousness* is:
1. "Uprightness"—in right standing with God.
2. Doing the right thing according to Biblical standards.
3. "Adherence or conformity to an established norm."

4. Virtuous.

5. Moral.

Throughout the Bible, mankind is corrupt and lacking in righteousness.

- Romans 3:23 says, "for all have sinned and fall short of the glory of God."
- Isaiah 64:6 says, "All of us have become like one who is unclean, and all our righteous acts are like filthy rags; we all shrivel up like a leaf, and like the wind our sins sweep us away" (NIV).
- Mark 5:20 says, "For I say to you, that unless your righteousness exceeds the righteousness of the scribes and Pharisees, you will by no means enter the kingdom of heaven."
- Galatians 2:21 says: "I do not set aside the grace of God, for if righteousness could be gained through the law, Christ died for nothing" (NIV).

Man is totally incapable of making himself righteous.

- Romans 3:19–20 says, "Obviously, the law applies to those to whom it was given, for its purpose is to keep people from having excuses and to bring the entire world into judgment before God. For no one can ever be made right in God's sight by doing what his law commands. For the more we know God's law, the clearer it becomes that we aren't obeying it" (NLT).

Only through the atoning work of Jesus Christ, the Son of the living God, can man receive righteousness.

- Isaiah 54:17 says, "No weapon formed against you shall prosper, and every tongue which rises against you in judgment You shall condemn. This is the heritage of the servants of the LORD, And their righteousness is from Me," Says the LORD."
- Isaiah 61:10 says, "I am overwhelmed with joy in the LORD my God! For he has dressed me with the clothing of salvation and draped me in a robe of righteousness. I am like a bridegroom in his wedding suit or a bride with her jewels" (NLT).
- Romans 5:17 says, "The sin of this one man, Adam, caused death to rule over us, but all who receive God's wonderful, gracious gift of righteousness

will live in triumph over sin and death through this one man, Jesus Christ" (NLT).

The imparting of righteousness is in two distinctive and inseparable phases:

Phase 1 Justification. In justification by faith man is made right with the demands of the law by the atonement of Christ.

2 Corinthians 5:21 says, "For He made Him who knew no sin to be sin for us, that we might become the righteousness of God in Him."

Phase 2 Sanctification. In sanctification man is progressively made righteous in character and conduct.

- 1 John 1:6–9 says, "If we say that we have fellowship with Him and yet walk in the darkness, we lie and do not practice the truth; but if we walk in the light as He Himself is in the light, we have fellowship with one another, and the blood of Jesus His Son cleanses us from all sin. If we say that we have no sin, we are deceiving ourselves, and the truth is not in us. If we confess our sins, He is faithful and righteous to forgive us our sins and to cleanse us from all unrighteousness" (NASB).
- Romans 6:19 says, "I am speaking in human terms because of the weakness of your flesh. For just as you presented your members as slaves to impurity and to lawlessness, resulting in further lawlessness, so now present your members as slaves to righteousness, resulting in sanctification" (NASB).
- Hebrews 12:14 says: "Pursue peace with all men, and the sanctification without which no one will see the Lord" (NASB).

3. Our Armor: Peace

Peace is a sense of well-being and fulfillment that comes from God and is dependent on His presence. Peace is a frequent word in both testaments used in a variety of ways. In the Old Testament times it was the usual word of greeting.

- Ephesians 6:15 says, "For shoes, put on the peace that comes from the Good News, so that you will be fully prepared" (NLT).

- Genesis 29:6 says, "How is he?" Jacob asked. "He's well and prosperous. Look, here comes his daughter Rachel with the sheep" (NLT).

Peace is also used throughout the Bible to indicate a spirit of tranquility and freedom from either inward or outward disturbance.

- Numbers 6:26 says, "May the LORD show you his favor and give you his peace" (NLT).
- 1 Kings 4:24–25 says: "Solomon's dominion extended over all the kingdoms west of the Euphrates River, from Tiphsah to Gaza. And there was peace throughout the entire land. Throughout the lifetime of Solomon, all of Judah and Israel lived in peace and safety" (NLT).
- Acts 9:31 says, "The church then had peace throughout Judea, Galilee, and Samaria, and it grew in strength and numbers. The believers were walking in the fear of the Lord and in the comfort of the Holy Spirit" (NLT).

When nations enjoyed peace, it was regarded as a gift from God.

- Leviticus 26:6 says, "I will give you peace in the land, and you will be able to sleep without fear. I will remove the wild animals from your land and protect you from your enemies" (NLT).
- Psalm 29:11 says, "The LORD will give strength to His people; The LORD will bless His people with peace."

Perhaps the word peace is most frequently used in both testaments to denote that spiritual tranquility which all can enjoy when through faith in Christ they are brought into a right relationship with God. There is the peace with God enjoyed by all truly regenerated persons (Romans 5:1 and Colossians 1:20) and the peace of God enjoyed only by believers who meet its conditions (Philippians 4:6–7). Perhaps both aspects of peace are implied in such passages as Isaiah 26:3 and John 14:27.

Christ came to provide peace on earth (Luke 2:14) but this will not be fully realized until He returns again to affect it in person.

- Isaiah 9:6–7 says, "For unto us a Child is born, unto us a Son is given; and the government will be upon His shoulder. And His name will be called Wonderful, Counselor, Mighty God, Everlasting Father, and Prince of Peace. Of the increase of His government and peace there will be no end."

- Isaiah 11:6–9 says, "In that day the wolf and the lamb will live together; the leopard and the goat will be at peace. Calves and yearlings will be safe among lions, and a little child will lead them all. The cattle will graze among bears. Cubs and calves will lie down together. And lions will eat grass as the livestock do. Babies will crawl safely among poisonous snakes. Yes, a little child will put its hand in a nest of deadly snakes and pull it out unharmed. Nothing will hurt or destroy in all my holy mountain. And as the waters fill the sea, so the earth will be filled with people who know the LORD" (NLT).
- Micah 4:3–4 says, "The LORD will settle international disputes. All the nations will beat their swords into plowshares and their spears into pruning hooks. All wars will stop, and military training will come to an end. Everyone will live quietly in their own homes in peace and prosperity, for there will be nothing to fear. The LORD Almighty has promised this" (NLT).

4. Our Armor: The Shield of Faith

Ephesians 6:16 says, "In every battle you will need faith as your shield to stop the fiery arrows aimed at you by Satan" (NLT)

Faith has a twofold sense in the Bible, an active and a passive one.

- Active: "fidelity—a faithful devotion to duty or one's obligations or vows; faithfulness; allegiance to some person or thing; loyalty, trustworthiness. An example of active faith is found in Romans 3:3, where "the faith of God" means His fidelity to promise.
- Passive: trust, reliance, complete trust, confidence, or reliance: as children, usually have *faith* in their parents.

In the Old Testament (KJV) the word *faith* occurs only twice (Deuteronomy 32:20, Habakkuk, 2:4), and even the verb form, *to believe* appears less than 30 times. What we find in the Old Testament is not so much a doctrine of faith, as examples of it. It sets forth the life of the servants of God as a life of faith. Old Testament faith is never mere ascent to a set of doctrines or outward acceptance of the Law, but utter confidence in the faithfulness of God and a consequent loving obedience to His will. In the Old Testament, faith was put in the Word of God spoken by the prophets because they spoke for God, and God is absolutely trustworthy.

- Exodus 19:9 says, "Then the LORD said to Moses, "I am going to come to you in a thick cloud so the people themselves can hear me as I speak to you. Then they will always have confidence in you." Moses told the LORD what the people had said" (NLT).

- 2 Chronicles 20:20 says, "So they rose early in the morning and went out into the Wilderness of Tekoa; and as they went out, Jehoshaphat stood and said, "Hear me, O Judah and you inhabitants of Jerusalem: Believe in the LORD your God, and you shall be established; believe His prophets, and you shall prosper."

New Testament writers tell us that the faith manifested by the Old Testament saints was not different in kind from that expected of Christians. In contrast with the extreme rarity with which the terms *faith* and *believe* are used in the Old Testament, they occur many times in the New Testament; about 500 times. The main reason for this is that the New Testament makes the claim that the promised Messiah had finally come to this earth, and, to the bewilderment of many, the form of the fulfillment did not obviously correspond to the Messianic promise. It required a real act of faith to believe that Jesus of Nazareth was the promised Messiah. It was not long after this that *to believe* meant to become a Christian—those who followed the teachings of Jesus Christ and believed He was the promised Messiah. In the New Testament, faith therefore becomes the supreme act of all human acts and experiences. In His miracles and teaching, Jesus aimed at creating in His disciples a complete trust in Him as the Messiah and Savior of the world. Everywhere He offered Himself as the object of faith, and made it plain that faith in Him was necessary for eternal life, and that refusal to accept His claims would bring eternal ruin or damnation. His primary concern with His 12 disciples was to build up their faith in Him as their Lord and Savior. Jesus Christ went about all of Jerusalem and the surrounding area to preach, teach and to heal. His 12 disciples and the apostles like Paul did just that! We, also, as His disciple here on this earth today should do likewise—go about preaching, teaching, and healing as He did!

It is recorded in the book of Acts that the first Christians called themselves "the believers."

- Acts 2:44 says, "And all the believers met together constantly and shared everything they had" (NLT). And these believers went everywhere persuading

91

others that Jesus was indeed the promised Messiah and bringing them unto obedience to the faith that is in Jesus.

- Acts 6:7 says, "Then the word of God spread, and the number of the disciples multiplied greatly in Jerusalem, and a great many of the priests were obedient to the faith."
- Acts 17:4 says, "Some of the Jews were persuaded and joined Paul and Silas, as did a large number of God-fearing Greeks and not a few prominent women" (NIV).
- Acts 28:24 says, "Some believed and some didn't" (NLT).

Before long, as communities of believers arose in various parts of the Mediterranean world, the meaning and implications of the Christian faith had to be taught them by the apostolic leaders, like Paul, Silas, and Stephen; and so the New Testament books appeared in written form known as the Gospels of Jesus Christ.

It is in Paul's epistles that the meaning of faith is most clearly and fully set forth. Faith is trust in the person of Jesus, the truth of His teaching, and the redemptive work He accomplished at Calvary, and as a result, a total submission to Him and His message, which are accepted as from God. Our faith is in Jesus as the eternal Son of God, the God-man, the second man Adam, who died in man's behalf, making possible justification with God, adoption into His family, sanctification, and ultimately glorification. His death brings redemption from all sin. The truth of His claims is attested by God's raising Him from the dead. It includes a radical and total commitment to Him as the Lord of one's life. In order to call yourself a Christian or a believer, one must develop an intimate relationship with Jesus Christ and make Him Lord of your life. Being a believer is all about a relationship not a religion! Our salvation is based upon our faith in what Jesus did for us before and after Calvary!

Unbelief, or a lack of faith in the Christian Gospel, appears everywhere in the New Testament as the supreme evil. Not to make a decisive response to God's offer in Christ would mean that the individual remains in his sin and is eternally lost. Faith alone can save Him. One cannot obtain salvation by doing good works or one's lineage.

The Biblical definition of faith is found in Hebrews 11:1: "Now faith is the substance of things hoped for, the evidence of things not seen." The NLT says,

"What is faith? It is the confident assurance that what we hope for is going to happen. It is the evidence of things we cannot yet see." Read all of Hebrews 11 for it is known as the faith chapter in the Bible and it tells about the faith of our Bible heroes. When we read this chapter faithfully our faith will be built up and we will be blessed! The Bible tells us in this chapter that without faith it is impossible to please God.

Romans 12:3 teaches us that God has given each of us a measure of faith when we surrender our hearts and lives to Him through faith in what His son Jesus did for us! So how do we get more faith? By reading, studying, meditating, memorizing, and obeying the Word of God. The more Word we have inside our hearts the more faith we will have in God and the things of God. The Bible tells us in Romans 10:17: "So then faith cometh by hearing, and hearing by the word of God" (KJV).

5. *Our Armor: The Helmet of Salvation*

Ephesians 6:17 NLT tells us to put on salvation as our helmet.

In the Bible the word *salvation* is not necessarily a technical, theological term, but simply denotes "deliverance" from almost any kind of evil, whether material or spiritual. Theologically, however, it denotes: the whole process by which man is delivered from all that interferes with the enjoyment of God's highest blessings. The actual enjoyment of those blessings—the root idea in salvation is deliverance from some danger or evil, defeating our adversary (the devil). Salvation delivers us from:

1. Trouble

- Psalm 34:6: "This poor man cried out, and the LORD heard him, and saved him out of all his troubles."
- Psalm 27:5: "For in the time of trouble He shall hide me in His pavilion; in the secret place of His tabernacle He shall hide me; He shall set me high upon a rock."
- Psalm 32:7: "You are my hiding place; you shall preserve me from trouble; you shall surround me with songs of deliverance. Selah"

2. Our Enemies

- Judges 8:34 NLT: "They forgot the LORD their God, who had rescued them from all their enemies surrounding them."
- 2 Samuel 3:18 NLT: "Now is the time! For the LORD has said, 'I have chosen David to save my people from the Philistines and from all their other enemies.'"
- Psalm 143:12 NIV: "In your unfailing love, silence my enemies; destroy all my foes, for I am your servant."

3. Violence or Violent Men

- 2 Samuel 22:3: "The God of my strength, in whom I will trust; my shield and the horn of my salvation, my stronghold and my refuge; My Savior, You save me from violence."
- Psalm 140:1: "Deliver me, O LORD, from evil men; Preserve me from violent men."

4. Reproach

- Psalm 57:3: "He shall send from heaven and save me; He reproaches the one who would swallow me up. Selah God shall send forth His mercy and His truth."
- Proverbs 14:34: "Righteousness exalts a nation, but sin is a reproach to any people.

5. Being exiled

- Psalm 106:47: "Save us, O LORD our God, and gather us from among the Gentiles, to give thanks to your holy name, To triumph in Your praise."
- Isaiah 51:14, NASB: "The exile will soon be set free, and will not die in the dungeon, nor will his bread be lacking."

6. Death

- Psalm 6:4–5: "Return, O LORD, deliver me! Oh, save me for your mercies' sake! For in death there is no remembrance of you; in the grave who will give you thanks?"

- Revelation 21:4: "And God will wipe away every tear from their eyes; there shall be no more death, nor sorrow, nor crying. There shall be no more pain, for the former things have passed away."

7. Sin

- Genesis 4:7, NIV: "If you do what is right, will you not be accepted? But if you do not do what is right, sin is crouching at your door; it desires to have you, but you must master it."
- Romans 6:14, NLT: "Sin is no longer your master, for you are no longer subject to the law, which enslaves you to sin. Instead, you are free by God's grace."

In the Old Testament, a complete and total trust in God was of the utmost importance to receive salvation. Next in importance was obedience to God's moral law as expressed in the various codes of law. But God was not satisfied with a legalistic fulfillment of the letter of the law, He required more from the believers. Forgiveness of sins was based upon repentance. Most sins also required a ritual sacrifice as part of the act of repentance, thus the animal sacrifices.

In the Gospels, the teachings of Jesus, salvation is often used to denote deliverance from trouble, like sickness or the spirit of infirmity.

- Matthew 9:22: "But Jesus turned around, and when He saw her He said, 'Be of good cheer, daughter; your faith has made you well.' And the woman was made well from that hour."

But salvation usually means deliverance from sin through repentance, acceptance, receiving, and believing in Jesus of Nazareth as our Savior and Lord.

The Plan of Salvation: ARBC Gospel

ADMIT

That sin is a problem in my life; I was born into sin, and I have a sinful nature. Man is a sinner: Romans 3:23 says, "for all have sinned and fall short of the glory of God."

God is a just God and must punish sin. 1 Peter 2:9 (NLT) says, "the Lord knows how to rescue godly people from their trials, even while punishing the wicked right up until the Day of Judgment." Sin's penalty is death. Romans 6: 23 says, "For the wages of sin is death, but the gift of God is eternal life in Christ Jesus our Lord." Man can't save himself, or earn his way into heaven. Ephesians 2:8–9 (NIV) says: "For it is by grace you have been saved, through faith—and this not from yourselves, it is the gift of God—not by works, so that no one can boast." The Bible tells us here that we cannot earn our way into heaven by doing good works. Just being a good person, living a moral life will not get you into heaven. Besides, how do you know when you have done enough good works to deserve God's reward of heaven! There is nothing we can do to earn our way into heaven. It is only by the grace of God and faith in His Son Jesus that we can obtain our eternal life. Our salvation is a free gift from God as we put our faith and trust in Jesus Christ as our Redeemer!

REPENT

Ask God to forgive you of all your sins and be willing to turn from all of them. **True repentance** means we sincerely ask God to forgive us of our sins, and then be determined to sin no more! True repentance involves turning away from sin and renouncing the devil and any acts of sin you have committed. Taking a 360 degree turnabout—turning away from sin and turning toward living a life that pleases our Lord!

- Matthew 3:1–2 says, "In those days John the Baptist came, preaching in the Desert of Judea and saying, 'Repent, for the kingdom of heaven is near.'"
- Jesus said in Matthew 4:17 "Repent, for the kingdom of heaven is near."
- Mark 1:14–15 says, "After John was put in prison; Jesus went into Galilee, proclaiming the good news of God. 'The time has come,' he said. 'The kingdom of God is near. Repent and believe the good news!'"
- Jesus said in Luke 13:3–5, "I tell you, no; but unless you repent you will all likewise perish."

BELIEVE

Jesus Christ is the solution—He is the answer to our sin problem. Believing on the Lord Jesus is essential to salvation. To believe on the Lord Jesus Christ means:

1. To believe that Jesus is the Son of God.

- Romans 10: 9: "For if you confess with your mouth that Jesus is Lord and believe in your heart that God raised him from the dead, you will be saved" (NLT).
- John 3:36: "Whoever believes in the Son has eternal life, but whoever rejects the Son will not see life, for God's wrath remains on him" (NIV).

2. To believe that Jesus alone can save.

- Acts 4:12: "There is salvation in no one else! There is no other name in all of heaven for people to call on to save them" (NLT).
- Hebrews 7:25: "Therefore he is able, once and forever, to save everyone who comes to God through him. He lives forever to plead with God on their behalf" (NLT).

3. To believe that Jesus took the penalty of our sin, which was death on the cross, upon himself.

- Romans 5:6–8: "You see, at just the right time, when we were still powerless, Christ died for the ungodly. Very rarely will anyone die for a righteous man, though for a good man someone might possibly dare to die. But God demonstrates his own love for us in this: While we were still sinners, Christ died for us" (NIV).
- Philippians 2:8: "And being found in appearance as a man, He humbled Himself by becoming obedient to the point of death, even death on a cross" (NASB).

4. To believe that Jesus purchased eternal life for us, which he offers as a free gift. This gift is received by faith alone, not by works.

- 1 John 5: 11–13: "And this is the testimony: God has given us eternal life, and this life is in his Son. He who has the Son has life; he who does not have the Son of God does not have life. I write these things to you who believe in the name of the Son of God so that you may know that you have eternal life" (NIV).

- Ephesians 2: 8–9: "For it is by grace you have been saved, through faith--and this not from yourselves, it is the gift of God; not by works, so that no one can boast" (NIV).
- What is faith? Trusting Jesus Christ alone for our salvation! John 3:16 tells us "For God so loved the world that he gave his one and only Son, that whoever believes in him shall not perish but have eternal life."

5. To believe that Jesus is able to save you and keep you.

- Hebrews 7:25: "Therefore He is also able to save to the uttermost those who come to God through Him (Jesus Christ), since He always lives to make intercession for them."

It is important for us to know and believe that Jesus sits at the right hand of the Father, right now, interceding for us. Before Jesus went to be with His heavenly Father after His resurrection, He asked the Father to keep us and care for us until we are united with them in heaven.

- John 17:11: "Now I am departing the world; I am leaving them behind and coming to you. Holy Father, keep them and care for them--all those you have given me--so that they will be united just as we are" (NLT).

CONFESS

Believing on the Lord Jesus Christ leads us to confession.

- 1 John 1:9: "If we confess our sins, He is faithful and just to forgive us our sins and to cleanse us from all unrighteousness."

There are two aspects of confession:

1. There is the confession or admission of your sins as you ask for forgiveness and pardon for your sins.
2. Then there is the testimony or confession to your friends, the making public of your faith and trust in Jesus Christ as your Lord and Savior.

If you will learn early in your Christian life that Christianity is not a "religion" but a daily sharing of all your thoughts and ideas with Christ Jesus—an intimate personal relationship with Him—then you will find that it becomes easy to speak to others about Him. No straining and striving—just a natural flow that comes from spending so much time with Him. Those whom you love you will want to spend time with. Thus, you become a witness for Him almost without realizing it or thinking about it.

It is vital that you open yourself up to this daily relationship. He will light up your life and that light will shine from you wherever you go, dispelling darkness. It is a privilege to allow Him to shine His light through and around you!

When you admit you are a sinner, truly repent, believe that Jesus is the solution to your sin problem and confess and accept Jesus as Lord and Savior, you are saved!

At this time I would like to invite you to **REPENT** (turn from your sins) and by faith **RECEIVE** Jesus Christ into your heart and life and follow Him in obedience as your Savior and Lord.

A SINNER'S PRAYER

Lord Jesus, I know that I am separated from God.
And I know that I have sinned against you.
I cannot cleanse away my own sins.
So come into my life today, Lord.
Cleanse me. I renounce all sin in my life.
Wash my sins away completely.
Forgive me. I surrender my heart and life to you Lord.
Do whatever you want to do with me.
I need you.
I want you in my heart. Come into my heart Lord Jesus.
Be my Lord and Master.
I open the door to my heart.
I receive you Lord right now as my Savior.
And make you Lord of my life today.
Here is my life.
Take me and use me for Your glory.
You are the potter and I am the clay.
Make me into a vessel of honor to be used by you.

Thank you for hearing my prayer, Lord.
Your forgiveness is wonderful.
Thank you for coming into my life today. Amen

Now that you have put on salvation as your helmet in order to grow in Christ and to become a new creature in Christ, you must communicate with Jesus through prayer and incorporating a life of fasting also. It is essential to your spiritual growth that you read your Bible and pray every day. As a new Christian, get connected to a full gospel church where the anointing of God is present. The Bible teaches us to gather together with other believers to praise, worship, and hear the Word preached and taught. You have begun a new adventure with Jesus as your Savior and Lord. As your relationship with Him grows and develops, you will live a very blessed and fulfilled life. As you allow the will of the Lord to be accomplished in your life and you are truly a servant of the Lord, God will transform you and make you into that vessel of honor which can be used by Him. Your destiny, God's purpose for you, will be revealed to you and you will become a blessing to others as you minister to their needs. Always put God first in all that you do and let love be the motivator for everything you do for Him!

6. Our Armor: The Sword of the Spirit and Prayer

Our only offensive weapon against the devil is to take the sword of the Spirit, which is the Word of God. This is how Jesus defeated Satan in *Matthew 4*—Jesus told the devil "it is written," and the enemy fled from him.

After we have put our armor on daily so that we don't go out into the world naked and vulnerable to the devil's schemes or tricks, we are to pray in the Holy Spirit according to the Word of God. Ephesians 6:18 tells us, "Pray at all times and on every occasion in the power of the Holy Spirit. Stay alert and be persistent in your prayers for all Christians everywhere" (NLT).

Praying in tongues is a power weapon against our enemy, the devil. It is a direct prayer line to our heavenly Father through the Son Jesus, who sits at the right hand of His Father making intercession for us! So we are to pray about everything no matter where we are or what we are going through, so that we can *stand* up against the wiles (to stand firm against all strategies and tricks of the devil).

We are supposed to be strong with the Lord's mighty power, and this means to stand in the midst of adversity with the armor of God provided for us in Ephesians 6:10–20. When we have put on this armor, we are equipped and ready to stand against whatever the devil slings at us today! Have you put on your armor today so that you can stand? Do it right now, and be ready and equipped to fight the enemy of our souls—the devil, Satan. Pray for courage and strength to stand when tests, trials and tribulation come. Be an overcomer by being ready to fight the battle and be victorious against your adversary with the Word of God coming out of your mouth. It is sharper than any two-edged sword, meaning it cuts when it goes in and cuts when it comes out. Hebrews 4:12 tells us, "For the word of God is full of living power. It is sharper than the sharpest knife, cutting deep into our innermost thoughts and desires. It exposes us for what we really are" (NLT).

Just remember that the Word of God (your sword) is the only offensive weapon you have against your adversary, the devil! Use it wisely and correctly at all times.

Lastly, we should ask God for holy boldness for ourselves and others like the apostle Paul did in Ephesians.

- Ephesians 6:19–21: "And pray for me, too. Ask God to give me the right words as I boldly (fearlessly) explain God's secret plan that the Good News is for the Gentiles, too. I am in chains now for preaching this message as God's ambassador. But pray that I will keep on speaking boldly (fearlessly) for him, as I should" (NLT). Thank you Lord for your armor and boldness to proclaim your Word with conviction!

Waiting on the Lord

Standing in the Presence of the Lord God Almighty sometimes involves *waiting*. The definition of *wait* according to Webster is:

Wait:
- To stay in a place or remain inactive or in anticipation until something expected takes place.
- To be ready or at hand; as, dinner is waiting for us.
- To remain temporarily undone or neglected: as, that work will have to wait.
- To hope for something.

Waiting:

- The act of one who waits; a period of waiting.

To wait on the Lord or to wait for the Lord to answer a prayer or need is not easy. In fact, it is most of the time very hard work especially if we are leaning on our own flesh. That is why it is so important that we depend upon the Holy Spirit to help us wait by standing in His presence or waiting while in the presence of the Lord. Waiting while in the presence of the Lord requires a lot of patience and we all know what patience brings if we pray for it—tribulation! So how do we get through tribulation of any kind graciously?

- By keeping our minds stayed on Him which gives us peace in the midst of the storm. (Isaiah 26:3)
- By not murmuring or complaining or arguing (Philippians 2:14)
- By staying in His presence through praise and worship. In everything give thanks! (1 Thessalonians 5:18)
- By walking daily in the Spirit and not in the flesh. (Galatians 5:16, 25).
- By being anointed to wait. Ask God to anoint you to wait while in His presence which makes waiting much easier. (Psalm 23:3).
- By being obedient to the Word of God and the Spirit of God. (Exodus 24:7).
- By doing the right thing all the time—living a holy or righteous life. (Hebrews 12:14).
- By listening to the voice of the Holy Spirit and not fulfilling the lust of our flesh.
- By making sacrifices and being a servant of the Lord—doing his will not our will.
- It's not about us, it is all about Him—what does He want us to do and say?
- And most importantly, praying all the time anywhere either in tongues with your prayer language or with the understanding (Ephesians 6:18).
- Pray out loud or silently, whatever you are most comfortable with or seems necessary at the time.
- PRAY! PRAY! PRAY! AND THEN PRAY SOME MORE!

So what does the Bible say about waiting on the Lord? God answers our prayers in one of three ways: no, yes, or wait—not now, but later, sometimes years later.

- Psalm 25:5: "Lead me in your truth and teach me, for you are the God of my salvation; On You I wait all the day." (NLT says "All day long I put my hope in you."

- Psalm 25:21: "Let integrity and uprightness preserve me, for I wait for you." NIV says, "May integrity and uprightness protect me, because my hope is in you."

- Psalm 27:14, KJV: "Wait on the LORD: be of good courage, and he shall strengthen thine heart: wait, I say, on the LORD." NLT: "Wait patiently for the LORD. Be brave and courageous. Yes, wait patiently for the LORD."

- Psalm 37:7, 9: "Rest in the LORD, and wait patiently for Him; Do not fret because of him who prospers in his way, Because of the man who brings wicked schemes to pass. V. 9: "For evildoers shall be cut off; But those who wait on the LORD, They shall inherit the earth."

- Psalm 37:34, NIV: "Wait for the LORD and keep his way. He will exalt you to inherit the land; when the wicked are cut off, you will see it."

- Psalm 59:9, NLT: "You are my strength; I wait for you to rescue me, for you, O God, are my place of safety.

- Psalm 62:5, NLT: "I wait quietly before God, for my hope is in him."

- Psalm 130:5, NIV: "I wait for the LORD, my soul waits, and in his word I put my hope."

- Proverbs 20:22, NLT: "Don't say, "I will get even for this wrong." Wait for the LORD to handle the matter."

- Isaiah 8:17, NIV: "I will wait for the LORD, who is hiding his face from the house of Jacob. I will put my trust in him."

- Isaiah 30:18, NLT: "But the LORD still waits for you to come to him so he can show you his love and compassion. For the LORD is a faithful God. Blessed are those who wait for him to help them."

- Isaiah 40:31: "But those who wait on the LORD Shall renew their strength; they shall mount up with wings like eagles, they shall run and not be weary, they shall walk and not faint."

- Micah 7:7: "Therefore I will look to the LORD; I will wait for the God of my salvation; My God will hear me."

- Romans 8:25, NLT: "But if we look forward to something we don't have yet, we must wait patiently and confidently."

- Galatians 5:5, NLT: "But we who live by the Spirit eagerly wait to receive everything promised to us who are right with God through faith."

- 1 Thessalonians 1:10: "and to wait for His Son from heaven, whom He raised from the dead, even Jesus who delivers us from the wrath to come."

Waiting is a very important part of standing in the presence of the Lord God Almighty. Nobody really likes waiting, but when we do it as part of standing in His presence it makes waiting more enjoyable and less of a hardship. There have been numerous times throughout this walk with the Lord that I have had to stand in His presence or was in the wait mode. Sometimes, with the help of the Holy Spirit, I was able to do so graciously. But those times when I was standing depending on my own strength to see me through and not standing in His presence it was a lot more difficult and frustrating.

I would like to share a few of these experiences when I had to stand in the presence of the Lord. The time that stands out in my mind and in my heart the most is when I was waiting for my healing from depression and the bipolar condition that I had. Boy, was that a long and laborious process. I dealt with this problem for over 20 years. Now the amazing thing about this whole thing is that 6 months after my husband Seth got saved I started to have these emotional issues. So where do you think these problems came from? Certainly not from the Lord. So this started manifesting itself in about November of 1980 and I wasn't delivered from this condition until July of 2004. During those 20 plus years of dealing with emotional highs and lows I had the opportunity to learn all about waiting in the presence of the Lord. Believe me those periods of time that I was standing while in the presence of the Lord were much easier and much more pleasant than when I was waiting with my own strength, and not depending on the Lord to help me. Was it hard? Was it difficult? Was it frustrating? Did it seem like God was not hearing me or was never going to answer my prayers? Yes, yes, and yes to all these questions. It seemed at the time that I was going to be in the wait mode forever. It seemed that God was nowhere to be found and He wasn't even hearing me or paying any attention to me from time to time during this season in my life. But God did come through for me and I did get a breakthrough in July of 2004! So yes, I do know what it is like to wait for God to move on my behalf. I believe I am a stronger Christian and more anointed now than I could ever imagine. Why? It was because I was persistent and remained faithful and obedient to the Word of God and the Spirit of God through this time of waiting or standing.

Another time when standing in His presence was prevalent in my life was when Seth had finally agreed with me that we were going to go to Israel and stay for three months. That was an adventure that I will always remember and cherish. Getting prepared to be gone for three months was very frustrating and bothersome for Seth, but not so much for me because Seth has always taken care of all our financial affairs and I don't really even think too much about them or get overly concerned about that. God has always been faithful and on time when it comes to what I need or even sometimes what I want. So during the time frame when we were preparing to stay away from home for three months, Seth shouldered all the weight of getting everything set up financially so that we could go. Many times he would come up with these "what if" scenarios. Well, I got real tired of hearing about all those what if this happens or what if that happens and just told him that most of those "what if" scenarios would probably never happen, and if they did we would deal with them when they happened.

One other time I recall having to wait upon the Lord to move is when my daughter Michelle went to Haiti to start up the orphanage of Destiny Village. Things are very slow in Haiti and progress is very slow, but after a few years of travailing, working, believing, trusting, obeying, and doing, God answered all of our prayers and much was accomplished while Michelle was there. It was not easy work and sometimes we wanted to quit, but God helped us endure those difficult times, and gave us much success in our labor for Him in Haiti. Destiny Village in Haiti is what it is today because of much prayer and fasting and waiting for God to answer our prayers. The Bible tells us in Isaiah 40:31: "But those who wait on the LORD shall renew their strength; they shall mount up with wings like eagles, they shall run and not be weary, they shall walk and not faint." So keep on waiting for the Lord to do whatever you believe He will do and He will come through for you as He did for me many times.

These are just a few times when I was required by God to wait for a prayer to be answered and I found out first-hand what it took to stand in His presence. There have been many other times when we were asked by God to wait or stand and we have gotten through them all victoriously. Hallelujah! Praise His holy name!

Closing Prayer

Our dear and precious Heavenly Father I pray right now that you will help and anoint us to stand or wait in your presence by doing those things that will make standing or waiting easier and more pleasant. We thank you and praise you for asking us to STAND right now! When we have done all that we know to do then it is time for us to stand in your presence for a while until our prayers are answered or we see a change take place in our problems, situations, or circumstances. You are an awesome, loving, forgiving, merciful, compassionate, passionate, and an attentive Father and we know that you do hear and will answer all of our prayers soon! Help us to wait or stand in your presence during those difficult times in our lives persevering joyfully and peacefully. Hallelujah! Thank you Jesus! Praise the Lord! Glory and honor to God the Father, Jesus the Son, and the Holy Spirit. In Jesus name we pray, Amen.

Chapter Six

Review Questions

1. Give the reference in the Bible where we can find the armor of God.

2. What are the different defensive parts of the armor that we are to put on daily to protect ourselves from the schemes of our enemy, Satan?
    1.)
    2.)
    3.)
    4.)
    5.)

3. What does the belt of truth consist of? Give three or four Scripture references to support your answer.

4. What are the different ways peace is used in the Bible? Give at least one Scripture reference for each.
    1.)
    2.)
    3.)
    4.)
    5.)

5. Faith has a twofold sense in the Bible. What are they and how would you differentiate between the two? Give two Scripture verses that are an example of each kind.
    1.)
    2.)

6. The Biblical definition of faith can be found in _____. Write and memorize this Scripture verse!

7. How do we increase our faith?

8. *Ephesians 6:17* tells us to put on _____ as our _____.

9. Give your definition of what salvation involves.

10. Do you feel comfortable presenting the plan of salvation to someone who does not know the Lord? How would you go about doing this?

11. A good method to present the plan of salvation to an unsaved person in your life is to remember the ARBC gospel plan. What do each one of these letters stand for?
    1.) A-
    2.) R-
    3.) B-
    4.) C-

12. What are the two aspects of confession?
    1.)
    2.)

13. Write a salvation prayer.

14. What is our only offensive weapon against the devil? Where is this found in the Bible?

15. Waiting, while standing in the presence of the Lord requires patience. And praying for patience brings tribulation. So how do we get through tribulation, trials and testing graciously?
    1.)
    2.)

3.)

4.)

5.)

6.)

7.)

8.)

16. What are the three ways that God answers our prayers?

    1.)

    2.)

    3.)

17. What does the Bible have to say about waiting?

18. Can you give an example from your own life about how you had to wait on the Lord?

The King of Glory—Jesus is the King of Glory

Review of Chapter Six

It is imperative that we put on the whole armor of God daily found in Ephesians 6:10–20. Our defensive weapons in our fight against our enemy are: the belt of truth, the breastplate of righteousness, shoes of peace, shield of faith, and the helmet of salvation. The one and only offensive weapon we have and all that we need is the Word of God. After all, isn't that what Jesus used in his wilderness experience in Mark 4? If it is good enough for Jesus, it is good enough for us! In this chapter I shared with you the ARBC plan of salvation. As born-again, spirit-filled believers, we need to pray in our prayer language and with the understanding and also ask God for boldness! We discussed how standing in the presence of an Almighty God involves waiting sometimes, which is not easy but requires patience to endure trials, tribulation, and testing. There are many Scripture verses that emphasize waiting on the Lord. I concluded this chapter on standing in the presence of the Lord with examples in my own life when I was required by God Almighty to wait! You probably have similar experiences also.

So Who is the King of Glory?

- Psalm 24:8–10 KJV: "Who is this King of glory? The LORD strong and mighty, the LORD mighty in battle. Lift up your heads, O ye gates; even lift them up, ye everlasting doors; and the King of glory shall come in. Who is this King of glory? The LORD of hosts, he is the King of glory. Selah."

The Lord Jesus Christ is the King of glory! The Lord strong and mighty; the Lord mighty in battle-the Lord of hosts; he is the King of glory. What does that mean that He is the Lord of hosts? He is the strong Lord, the mighty Lord of battle, and the Lord of hosts (vs. 8, 10). Exodus 15:3 NLT tells us that the Lord is a warrior; yes, the LORD is his name! He is a warrior-a fighter, a fighting man, a man of war, a man experienced in war or battle. The Lord is the captain of a host (angels, heavenly beings) which he commands. Jesus is the King of glory!

In John 1:14, John speaks to us about how they (the disciples) saw the glory of the Lord:

- "And the Word became flesh and dwelt among us, and we beheld His glory, the glory as of the only begotten of the Father, full of grace and truth."
- "So the Word became human and lived here on earth among us. He was full of unfailing love and faithfulness. And we have seen his glory, the glory of the only Son of the Father" (NLT).

The Bible tells us that Jesus would suffer in many ways before entering his time of glory. Luke 24:26 NLT says: "Wasn't it clearly predicted by the prophets that the Messiah would have to suffer all these things before entering his time of glory?"

The twelve disciples of Jesus saw Jesus walking and operating in the glory realm. John 2:11 NLT says: "This miraculous sign at Cana in Galilee was Jesus' first display of his glory. And his disciples believed in him."

Jesus told his friend Martha that if she believed in Him as the Messiah who raised her brother Lazarus from the dead, she would see the glory of God. John 11:40 says: "Jesus said to her, "Did I not say to you that if you would believe you would see the glory of God?"

Jesus wanted his twelve closest and dearest friends to see His glory given to him by his heavenly Father. In John 17:24 NLT: Jesus prayed to His heavenly Father and said "Father, I want these whom you've given me to be with me, so they can see my glory. You gave me the glory because you loved me even before the world began!"

The apostle Paul was blinded by a bright light (the glory of God) on the way to Damascus. Acts 22:11 NLT says: "I was blinded by the intense light and had to be led into Damascus by my companions."

Once again, the Bible speaks about the rewards of obedience and the curses that follow a person who is disobedient. Romans 2:7–8 NLT says: "He will give eternal life to those who persist in doing what is good, seeking after the glory and honor and immortality that God offers. But he will pour out his anger and wrath on those who live for themselves, who refuse to obey the truth and practice evil deeds."

The Bible also admonishes us here to seek after the glory! Why should we seek after or desire to see the glory of the Lord manifested to us? Because it is in the glory realm that Jesus shows up and miracles are received. Besides, in this glory realm we experience the fullness of God's love, peace, and joy. In the glory realm, the Holy Spirit has liberty to save the lost, set the captives free from all bondages, and heal the sick! Many good and marvelous things happen when we are in the presence of the Lord God Almighty. Miracles take place in the glory realm!

The New Testament gospels have much to say about the King of glory—Jesus! The different names given to Jesus in the Bible tell us how great, mighty and glorious He was and is. Jesus said of Himself, "I am the Christ:"

- Matthew 16:20: "Then He commanded His disciples that they should tell no one that He was Jesus the Christ."
- Matthew 24:4: "For many will come in My name, saying, 'I am the Christ,' and will deceive many."
- Matthew 26:63–64 NIV: "But Jesus remained silent. The high priest said to him, "I charge you under oath by the living God: Tell us if you are the Christ, the Son of God." "Yes, it is as you say," Jesus replied. "But I say to all of you: In the future you will see the Son of Man sitting at the right hand of the Mighty One and coming on the clouds of heaven."
- John 10:24–25: "Then the Jews surrounded Him and said to Him, 'How long do You keep us in doubt? If You are the Christ, tell us plainly.' Jesus answered them, 'I told you, and you do not believe. The works that I do in My Father's name, they bear witness of Me.'"

In Matthew 16:15–17 NLT, Jesus asked his disciples who they thought He was. "Then he asked them, 'Who do you say I am?' Simon Peter answered, 'You are the Messiah, the Son of the living God.' Jesus replied, 'You are blessed, Simon son of John, because my Father in heaven has revealed this to you. You did not learn this from any human being.'"

In Matthew 27:43, Jesus told others that He was the son of God. "He trusted in God; let Him deliver Him now if He will have Him; for He said, 'I am the Son of God.'"

Jesus called Himself *I am* in Mark 14:62. "Jesus said, 'I am. And you will see the Son of Man sitting at the right hand of the Power, and coming with the clouds of heaven.'"

Jesus called Himself *the bread of life* in John 6:35. "And Jesus said to them, 'I am the bread of life. He who comes to me shall never hunger, and he who believes in me shall never thirst.'"

Jesus said He was *the living bread* in John 6:51. "I am the living bread which came down from heaven. If anyone eats of this bread, he will live forever; and the bread that I shall give is my flesh, which I shall give for the life of the world."

Jesus referred to Himself as *the light of the world* in John 8:12. "Then Jesus spoke to them again, saying, 'I am the light of the world. He who follows Me shall not walk in darkness, but have the light of life.'"

Jesus told his disciples in John 8:23 that He was from above, and not of this world. "And He said to them, 'You are from beneath; I am from above. You are of this world; I am not of this world.'"

Again in John 9:5 Jesus calls Himself *the light of the world*. "As long as I am in the world, I am the light of the world."

Jesus said in John 10:7–9 that He was *the door*:

- "Then Jesus said to them again, 'Most assuredly, I say to you, I am the door of the sheep. All who ever came before me are thieves and robbers, but the sheep did not hear them. I am the door. If anyone enters by me, he will be saved, and will go in and out and find pasture.'"
- Again Jesus declared He was *the door* in John 10:9: "I am the door. If anyone enters by me, he will be saved, and will go in and out and find pasture."

Jesus told his friend in John 10:11:

- "I am the good shepherd. The good shepherd lays down his life for the sheep."
- He told them again in John 10:14 about how He was the good shepherd to His sheep: "I am the good shepherd; I know my own sheep, and they know me."

Jesus wanted to know why the new believers called Him a blasphemer when He was not. "Why do you call it blasphemy when the Holy One who was sent into the world by the Father says, 'I am the Son of God?'" (John 10:30–36)

To reproach or to bring a railing accusation against anyone is bad enough, but to speak lightly or carelessly of God is a mortal sin. In Israel the punishment for blasphemy was death by stoning (see Leviticus 24:10–16).

In John 11:25–26, Jesus told Martha: "I am the resurrection and the life. Those who believe in me, even though they die like everyone else, will live again. They are given eternal life for believing in me and will never perish. Do you believe this, Martha?"

Jesus told the crowd in John 12:32: "And when I am lifted up on the cross, I will draw everyone to myself."

Jesus explained to His disciples while at a foot washing that He was a teacher (rabbi) and their Lord: "You call me Teacher and Lord, and you say well, for so I am" (John 13:13).

In John 14:6, Jesus told Thomas that He was the only way to get to heaven. "Jesus said to him, 'I am the way, the truth, and the life. No one comes to the Father except through me.'"

Jesus said He was the vine in John 15:1, 5: "I am the true vine, and My Father is the vinedresser." In verse 5 Jesus said: "I am the vine, you are the branches. He who abides in me, and I in him, bears much fruit; for without me you can do nothing."

Jesus told Paul in his Damascus experience that he was Jesus. "So I answered, 'Who are You, Lord?' And He said to me, 'I am Jesus of Nazareth, whom you are persecuting'" (Acts 22:8).

While John was on the island of Patmos in Greece, he was caught up in the spirit and Jesus told him that He was the alpha and the omega. "I was in the Spirit on the Lord's Day, and I heard behind me a loud voice, as of a trumpet, saying, 'I am the Alpha and the Omega, the First and the Last, the Beginning and the End,' says the Lord, 'who is and who was and who is to come, the Almighty'" (Revelation 1:8).

In Revelation 1:17–18 NLT, Jesus laid His hand on John and said He was the first and the last. "When I saw him, I fell at his feet as dead. But he laid his right hand on me and said, 'Don't be afraid! I am the First and the Last. I am the living one who died. Look, I am alive forever and ever! And I hold the keys of death and the grave.'"

Jesus also said that He was coming like a thief in the night—no one will know when He is coming, so we must be ready and looking for Him. "Behold, I am coming as a thief. Blessed is he who watches, and keeps his garments, lest he walks naked and they see his shame" (Revelation 16:15).

Jesus told us in Revelation 22:7, 12–13: He was coming quickly and we would be rewarded for our good works or deeds we have done here on earth. In verse 7, Jesus said: "Behold, I am coming quickly! Blessed is he who keeps the words of the prophecy of this book." In verses 12 and 13, He said: "And behold, I am coming quickly, and my reward is with me, to give to every one according to his work. I am the Alpha and the Omega, the Beginning and the End, the First and the Last."

In Revelation 22:16 NIV, Jesus called himself *the root and offspring of David*, and *the bright morning star*: "I, Jesus, have sent my angel to give you this testimony for the churches. I am the Root and the Offspring of David, and the bright Morning Star."

John, who was a witness to all that was written in the book of Revelation, wrote the final words of Jesus which were that He was coming soon! "He who is the faithful witness to all these things says, 'Yes, I am coming soon!' Amen! Come, Lord Jesus" (Revelation 22:20 NLT). So once again my question to you is are you ready and looking for Him to return?

All these *I am's* to which Jesus refers to Himself tell us who He Himself said He was and reveals that He was and still is the King of glory. Someday very soon that King of glory will return in all His splendor and majesty and come get His children—His bride! Are you His bride and are you ready?

The Miracles of Jesus Manifested His Glory

Jesus manifested His glory through the miracles He performed during His three years of public ministry. John 2:11 says: "This beginning of signs Jesus did in Cana of Galilee, and manifested His glory; and His disciples believed in Him." The first miracle Jesus performed was the turning the water into wine at a wedding in Cana.

The Miracles of Jesus in the Book of Matthew

We will consider the miracles of Jesus as they were recorded in the book of Matthew, who was one of Jesus' disciples. He was a tax collector called by Jesus to be an apostle (Matthew 9:9; 10:3). His accounts of the glory of the King of the Jews are:

- Jesus heals the leper in Matthew 8:1–3.
- Jesus healed Peter's mother-in-law and all those who were sick in Matthew 8:14–16.
- In Matthew 8:22–27 Jesus spoke to the wind and calmed the sea when a storm arose.
- In Matthew 8:28–34 Jesus commanded the demons to come out of people and they obeyed Him because He had that authority.
- In Matthew 9:1–8 Jesus healed a paralytic!
- In Matthew 9:18–25 Jesus raised a girl from the dead and healed a woman with a bleeding problem for twelve years
- Jesus healed the blind and mute (delivers a demon-possessed man) in Matthew 9:27–34.
- Jesus fed five thousand plus people with five loaves of bread and two fish in Matthew 14:13–21.
- Jesus walked on the water on the Sea of Galilee in Matthew 14:22–33.
- All those who touched his garment were healed in Matthew 14:34–36.
- Jesus honored the faith of the Canaanite woman in Matthew 15:21–28.
- In Matthew 15:29–38 NIV, Jesus fed over four thousand people with only seven loaves of bread and a few small fish.
- In Matthew 17:14–21 Jesus healed a boy who had seizures or epilepsy.

- In Matthew 20:29–34 Jesus healed two blind men who sat by the roadside for many years. This is the last recorded miracle by Jesus in the book of Matthew.

The Miracles of Jesus in the Book of Mark

The glory of our King Jesus was also revealed in the book of Mark who portrays Jesus as a strong man of great energy, constantly on the move. Stories of the miracles Jesus performed make up the bulk of the Gospel according to Mark—exorcisms, healings, feeding crowds and walking on water. Words like "amazing" and "astonishing" are the words Mark often used to describe the people's reactions to Jesus. So here are the recorded miracles that The King of Kings performed according to the apostle Mark:

- The first miracle Jesus of Nazareth performed according to the apostle Mark was in Capernaum on the Sabbath in the synagogue where He delivered a man possessed with an evil spirit (Mark 1:21–28).
- In Mark 1:29–34 Jesus healed Simon's mother-in-law of a fever and He also healed many others.
- Jesus healed a man with leprosy in Mark 1:40–45.
- Jesus healed a paralytic in Mark 2:1–5.
- In Mark 4:35–41 Jesus calmed the storm.
- Jesus set a demon-possessed man free from a "Legion" of evil spirits in Mark 5:1–13.
- In Mark 5:21–43 Jesus raised the daughter of Jairus from the dead, and on the way to his house He also healed a woman with an issue of blood for twelve years.
- Jesus feeds the five thousand in Mark 6:30–44.
- Jesus walked on the water in Mark 6:45–56.
- Jesus healed a deaf and mute man in Mark 7:31–37.
- Jesus fed a crowd of more than four thousand with seven loaves of bread and a few fish in Mark 8:1–10.
- Jesus healed a blind man at Bethsaida by spitting on the man's eyes in Mark 8:22–26.
- Jesus delivered a boy from a deaf and dumb spirit in Mark 9:14–29. His disciples wanted to know why they could not drive the spirit out. Jesus' answer was that this kind comes out only by prayer and fasting.

- Blind Bartimaeus received his sight in Mark 10:46–52; the blind man's faith healed him.

So these are the recorded incidences in the book of Mark of how Jesus our Lord and Savior showed us His glory by doing these miracles.

The Miracles of Jesus in the Book of Luke

We will now look into the book of Luke to see the glory of our Lord and Savior as we contemplate the miracles He did in this gospel. Luke's Gospel is the longest of the four Gospels and presents Jesus as the Savior of the world; it highlights the ministry of the Holy Spirit; and it pays particular attention to women, children, the poor, and the oppressed. The central theme of the book of Luke is that nothing is impossible with God. Luke, a physician, writes with the compassion and warmth of a family doctor as he carefully documents the perfect humanity of the Son of Man, Jesus Christ. Luke is the author of this third Gospel and the *Book of Acts* in the New Testament, and a close friend and traveling companion of Paul's. Because he was a Gentile and a Greek, his perspective of miracles of Jesus was somewhat different. So, here are the miracles of Jesus from Nazareth as recorded by Luke:

- The first recorded miracle that Jesus performed in Luke's Gospel is in Luke 4:31–37, where our Lord drove out an evil spirit from a man who was possessed by the devil. These verses of Scripture tell us that Jesus taught the people about the Kingdom of God with authority. The people were amazed how Jesus of Nazareth, with authority and power, gave orders to evil spirits and they came out of those He prayed for!
- Luke tells us in Luke 4:38–41 that Jesus healed Simon's mother-in-law who had been suffering from a high fever and many others too. "And while the sun was setting, all who had any sick with various diseases brought them to Him; and laying His hands on every one of them, He was healing them. And demons also were coming out of many" (Luke 4:40–41 NASB).
- Jesus heals a paralytic in Luke 5:17–26

The following verses tell us that the power of the Lord was present for Jesus to heal the sick. All the people were amazed at how Jesus had the power to heal the sick and they gave glory to God. "Everyone was amazed and gave praise to God.

They were filled with awe and said, 'We have seen remarkable things today'" (Luke 5:26, NIV).

- The Faith of the Centurion in Luke 7:1–10.
- Jesus raised a widow's son in a town called Nain in Luke 7:11–17.
- Jesus calmed the storm on the Sea of Galilee in Luke 7:22–25.
- The healing of a Demon-possessed man in the region of the Gadarenes in Luke 8:26–37.
- In Luke 8:40–56 Jesus raised Jairus' daughter from the dead and on his way to Jairus' house he also healed a woman who had an issue of blood for twelve years.
- In Luke 9:10–17 when the crowds learned about the miracles Jesus and his disciples were performing they followed them. Jesus welcomed them and spoke to them about the kingdom of God and healed those who needed healing. He also fed five thousand people on five loaves of bread and two fish. All the people ate and were satisfied, and the disciples picked up twelve basketfuls of broken pieces that were left over.
- The healing of a boy with an evil spirit in Luke 9:37–43.
- After Jesus had cast out a demon from a man who was mute in Luke 11:14–24, the people accused Him of being possessed by an evil spirit.
- A crippled woman was healed (spirit of infirmity) by Jesus on the Sabbath in Luke 13:10–13.
- Ten men were healed of leprosy in Luke 17:11–19.
- In Luke 18:35–43 as Jesus approached Jericho, a blind man was sitting by the roadside begging and the Lord healed him!

These are the miracles recorded by Luke, the follower and disciple of Jesus which demonstrate to us the amazing power and glory of our Lord.

The Miracles of Jesus in the Book of John

In the Gospel according to John, we find these miracles which bring glory and honor to our Lord Jesus Christ:

- Jesus' very first miracle was at a wedding in Cana when he turned the water into wine in John 2:1–11.

- Some time later in John 4:1–15, Jesus went up to Jerusalem for a feast of the Jews. Sitting near the Sheep Gate lay a crippled man who was not able to get into the pool. This man had been an invalid for 38 years and had no one to help him into the pool. But Jesus healed this man!
- Jesus fed five thousand people with five barley loaves and two small fish in John 6:1–13.
- Jesus walked on the water in John 6:16–21.
- Jesus healed a man born blind in John 9:1–12.
- Jesus raised his friend Lazarus from the dead in John 11:1–44. This is an awesome display of the power that our Lord and Savior possessed during his three years of ministry on this earth.
- Jesus and the miraculous catch of fish in John 21:1–14.

These are the seven miracles recorded in the Gospel of John witnessed by his disciple John which reveal to us the glory and power of our Lord and Savior Jesus Christ of Nazareth.

These are the recorded times that Jesus performed miracles in the four Gospels. Many of them are the same accounts only written by a different apostle or disciple as he witnessed them with his own eyes. Jesus did these acts of kindness for the people because when He saw the needs of the people He was moved with compassion (Matthew 14:14). Each one of these recorded miracles reveals to us the glory and power of our Lord and Savior Jesus Christ.

The Seven *I Ams* of Jesus

1. Jesus—I Am the Bread of Life

- John 6:30–51 NASB says: "They said therefore to Him, "What then do you do for a sign that we may see, and believe you? What work do you perform? Our fathers ate the manna in the wilderness; as it is written, 'He gave them bread out of heaven to eat.' Jesus therefore said to them, 'Truly, truly, I say to you, it is not Moses who has given you the bread out of heaven, but it is My Father who gives you the true bread out of heaven. For the bread of God is that which comes down out of heaven, and gives life to the world.' They said therefore to Him, 'Lord, evermore give us this bread.' Jesus said to them, 'I am the bread of life; he who comes to me shall not hunger, and he who believes in me shall never thirst. But I said to you, that you have seen me, and yet do not believe. All that the Father gives me shall come to me, and the one who comes to me I will certainly not cast out. For I have come down from heaven, not to do My own will, but the will of Him who sent Me. And this is the will of Him who sent Me, that of all that He has given Me I lose nothing, but raise it up on the last day. For this is the will of My Father, that everyone who beholds the Son and believes in Him, may have eternal life; and I Myself will raise him up on the last day.' The Jews therefore were grumbling about Him, because He said, 'I am the bread that came down out of heaven.' And they were saying, 'Is not this Jesus, the son of Joseph, whose father and mother we know? How does He now say, 'I have come down out of heaven?' Jesus answered and said to them, 'Do not grumble among yourselves. No one can come to me, unless the Father who sent me draws him; and I will raise him up on the last day. It is written in the prophets, 'and they shall all be taught of God.' Everyone who has heard and learned from the Father, comes to Me. Not that any man has seen the Father, except the One who is from God; He has seen the Father. Truly, truly, I say to you, he who believes has eternal life. I am the bread of life. Your fathers ate the manna in the wilderness, and they died. This is the bread which comes down out of heaven, so that one may eat of it and not die. I am the living bread that came down out of heaven; if anyone eats of this bread, he shall live forever; and the bread also which I shall give for the life of the world is my flesh.'"

2. Jesus—I Am the Light of the World

- John 8:12–19 NLT says: "Jesus said to the people, 'I am the light of the world. If you follow me, you won't be stumbling through the darkness, because you will have the light that leads to life.' The Pharisees replied, 'You are making false claims about yourself!' Jesus told them, 'These claims are valid even though I make them about myself. For I know where I came from and where I am going, but you don't know this about me. You judge me with all your human limitations, but I am not judging anyone. And if I did, my judgment would be correct in every respect because I am not alone—I have with me the Father who sent me. Your own law says that if two people agree about something, their witness is accepted as fact. I am one witness, and my Father who sent me is the other.' 'Where is your father?' they asked. Jesus answered,

'Since you don't know who I am, you don't know who my Father is. If you knew me, then you would know my Father, too.'"

3. *Jesus—I Am the Door*

- John 10:7–10 says: "Then Jesus said to them again, 'Most assuredly, I say to you, I am the door of the sheep. All who ever came before me are thieves and robbers, but the sheep did not hear them. I am the door. If anyone enters by me, he will be saved, and will go in and out and find pasture. The thief does not come except to steal, and to kill, and to destroy. I have come that they may have life, and that they may have it more abundantly.'"

4. *Jesus—I Am the Good Shepherd*

- John 10:11–19 NLT says: "I am the good shepherd. The good shepherd lays down his life for the sheep. A hired hand will run when he sees a wolf coming. He will leave the sheep because they aren't his and he isn't their shepherd. And so the wolf attacks them and scatters the flock. The hired hand runs away because he is merely hired and has no real concern for the sheep. I am the good shepherd; I know my own sheep, and they know me, just as my Father knows me and I know the Father. And I lay down my life for the sheep. I have other sheep, too, that are not in this sheepfold. I must bring them also, and they will listen to my voice; and there will be one flock with one shepherd. The Father loves me because I lay down my life that I may have it back again. No one can take my life from me. I lay down my life voluntarily. For I have the right to lay it down when I want to and also the power to take it again. For my Father has given me this command. When he said these things, the people were again divided in their opinions about him."

5. *Jesus—I Am the Resurrection and the Life*

- John 11:25–26 says: "Jesus said to her, 'I am the resurrection and the life. He who believes in me, though he may die, he shall live. And whoever lives and believes in me shall never die. Do you believe this?'"

6. Jesus—I Am the Way, the Truth and the Life

- John 14:6–21 says: "Jesus said to him, 'I am the way, the truth, and the life. No one comes to the Father except through Me. If you had known me, you would have known My Father also; and from now on you know Him and have seen Him.' Philip said to Him, 'Lord, show us the Father, and it is sufficient for us.' Jesus said to him, 'Have I been with you so long and yet you have not known Me, Philip? He who has seen me has seen the Father; so how can you say, 'Show us the Father?' Do you not believe that I am in the Father, and the Father in Me? The words that I speak to you I do not speak on my own authority; but the Father who dwells in me does the works. Believe me that I am in the Father and the Father in Me, or else believe me for the sake of the works themselves. Most assuredly, I say to you, he who believes in me, the works that I do he will do also; and greater works than these he will do, because I go to My Father. And whatever you ask in my name, that I will do, that the Father may be glorified in the Son. If you ask anything in my name, I will do it. If you love me, keep my commandments. And I will pray the Father, and He will give you another Helper, that He may abide with you forever; the Spirit of truth, whom the world cannot receive, because it neither sees Him nor knows Him; but you know Him, for He dwells with you and will be in you. I will not leave you orphans; I will come to you. A little while longer and the world will see me no more, but you will see me. Because I live, you will live also. At that day you will know that I am in My Father and you in me, and I in you. He who has my commandments and keeps them, it is he who loves me. And he who loves me will be loved by My Father, and I will love him and manifest myself to him.'"

7. Jesus—I Am the True Vine

- John 15:1–10 says: "I am the true vine, and My Father is the vinedresser. Every branch in Me that does not bear fruit He takes away; and every branch that bears fruit He prunes, that it may bear more fruit. You are already clean because of the word which I have spoken to you. Abide in Me, and I in you. As the branch cannot bear fruit of itself, unless it abides in the vine, neither can you, unless you abide in Me. I am the vine, you are the branches. He who abides in me, and I in him, bears much fruit; for without me you can do nothing. If anyone does not abide in me, he is cast out as a branch and is withered; and they gather them and throw them into the fire, and they are burned. If you abide in me, and my words abide in you, you will ask what you desire, and it shall be done for you. By this My Father is glorified, that you bear much fruit; so you will be my disciples. As the Father loved Me, I also have loved you; abide in my love. If you keep my commandments, you will abide in my love, just as I have kept My Father's commandments and abide in His love."

These are the seven *I Ams* recorded in the Gospel of John written by John an apostle and disciple of Jesus. In each one Jesus revealed who He was, thus showing us how the Father honored and glorified the Son!

The Definition of Almighty

My definition of *almighty* describes who God was, is and will be to us when we stand in awe of Him in His presence. A God that is all powerful has all authority in heaven and earth, is always with us, and is everywhere at all times. He is a God who simply spoke the world into existence and made us to glorify Him. There is no other god like Him and He is all together lovely to me! He holds the world in His hands and is the master controller of this universe which He created. He is all powerful—A God who is to be feared (respected), praised, worshiped and admired by all. He is an awesome Father! I believe He is a sovereign God and He rules and reigns over the entire world. He is *El-Elyon*—the Highest Sovereign of the heavens and the earth!

My goal is to spend as much time as humanly possible in the presence of an Almighty God! I challenge you to do the same with the Lord's help. So I conclude this book on *The Glory of the Lord God Almighty* with this Scripture.

- 2 Corinthians 3:18 NIV: "And we, who with unveiled faces all reflect the Lord's glory, are being transformed into his likeness with ever-increasing glory, which comes from the Lord, who is the Spirit."
- NLT: "and all of us have had that veil removed so that we can be mirrors that brightly reflect the glory of the Lord. And as the Spirit of the Lord works within us, we become more and more like him and reflect his glory even more."

Take refuge in His Presence and reflect his glory by living a sanctified life!

Conclusion

The church is called to be a manifestation of God's glory. As part of the body of Christ, does your life manifest the glory of the Lord God Almighty? If not, why not?

Chapter Seven

Review Questions

1. According to Psalm 24:8–10 who is the King of Glory?

2. What did Jesus call himself in the four gospels? Give at least seven ways He described himself and also give the Scripture references.
    1.)
    2.)
    3.)
    4.)
    5.)
    6.)
    7.)

3. What are some of the miracles that Jesus performed according to Matthew? Give the Bible verse in Matthew that tells about each miracle.
    1.)
    2.)
    3.)
    4.)
    5.)
    6.)
    7.)

4. The glory of Jesus was also revealed in the book of Mark. List at least seven miracles of Jesus according to Mark's gospel and the chapter and verse where that miracle can be found.
    1.)

2.)

3.)

4.)

5.)

6.)

7.)

5. List seven miracles in the book of Luke and the reference for each of these miracles of our Lord.

1.)

2.)

3.)

4.)

5.)

6.)

7.)

6. John is my favorite gospel which also records the miracles that Jesus performed during his three years of public ministry. List seven miracles and their references that Jesus did according to his disciple John.

1.)

2.)

3.)

4.)

5.)

6.)

7.)

7. The four gospels record the same miracles that Jesus performed how are they different?

8. Which of the many miracles that Jesus did would you consider your favorite? Why?

9. How many miracles and how many *I Am* statements are recorded in the book of John?

10. List the seven *I Am* statements made by Jesus written in John's gospel and give the reference for each one. I recommend that you memorize these seven *I Ams.*

    1.)

    2.)

    3.)

    4.)

    5.)

    6.)

    7.)

11. How would you describe the glory of God Almighty? Is this something you seek after and desire in your life?

Printed in the United States
By Bookmasters